ON '

On the Waterfront

Maritime stories from Swansea, Port Talbot and other South Wales ports

Gareth A. Mills

First impression — November 1994

ISBN 1 85902 037 2

Printed by
J. D. Lewis & Sons Ltd.,
Llandysul, Dyfed.

To my three children
Susan, Jonathan and Fiona

Acknowledgements

The help, advice and co-operation of the following institutions and individuals is gratefully acknowledged:

South Wales Evening Post

Hugh Berlyn (Editor); Nick Carter (former Editor); George Edwards (Deputy Editor) and other staff, particularly Len Pitson (former Chief Photographer).

Associated British Ports: Swansea and Port Talbot

A. R. Klinck (Port Manager); R. Collins (Assistant Port Manager); J. S. Pope (Port Engineer); Capt. M. J. Ingamells (Dock and Harbour Master); Ian Rogerson (Properties & General Assistant); Mrs. Ingrid Davies (former Personnel Manager) and the Swansea and Port Talbot Pilots.

Associated British Ports: Cardiff

B. J. Harding (Port Manager); D. J. Harrison (Assistant Port Manager/Port Engineer); Capt. R. S. Grubb (Dock & Harbour Master); John Phelps (Administration Manager); Doug Jones former Administration Officer) and Miss Elizabeth Taylor (Senior Estates Clerk).

Alexandra Towing Company: Swansea

Patrick Lyons (Manager) and his staff.

Eddie King (retired Operations Officer, Swansea Docks); Bill King (retired Port Manager, Swansea & Port Talbot); Trevor Phillips (retired Assistant Port Manager Swansea & Port Tablot); Capt. T. E. W. Boyd (retired Docks & Harbour Master, Swansea); Charles L. Thomas (former Lord Mayor of Swansea); John Hughes (Local Studies Librarian) and staff of the Swansea Central Reference Library; Mrs J. M. Thomas; W. C. Rogers; John Barnes; Thomas Clarke; Carl Smith (Sou'wester Books); Malcolm Lewis; Bernard Davies; W. B. Perkins; Brian Murphy; Ken Richards; Graham Jones; Andrew Moulding; W. M. Hollister; Terry & Mrs Crockford; Colliers Photographic Emporium, Swansea; Bob & Julie Harris; Swansea Maritime & Industrial Museum; The National Maritime Museum, London; Burgess & Company, Swansea; Hubert Joseph (former Manager of the Britannia Steam Towing Co., Swansea); the late T. H. Richards; the late Douglas D. Harris; the late Tal. F. Jones; the late D. Gow; the late D. G. Holman; the late M. A. Clare; the late Charles Gant; Mrs T. Burrington; Capt. Bill Sparks; Lamport & Holt Line Ltd., Liverpool; Mr Derek Scott; the late W. T. Williams; Craig J. M. Carter (former Editor *Sea Breezes*); Philip Kershaw; the staff of Harrison Bros. Ltd., Uplands, Swansea.

The following books, journals and papers were also consulted: Duncan Haws, *Merchant Fleets* series, T. C. L. Publications—*Blue Funnel Line*, No. 6, 1984, *Shaw, Savill & Albion*, No. 10, 1987, *Cunard Line*, No. 12, 1987, *Blue Star Line*, No. 14, 1988, *Thos. & Jas. Harrison*, No. 15, 1988, *Ellerman Lines*, No. 16, 1989 and *Glen & Shire Lines*, No. 22, 1991; Grahame Farr, *Wreck and Rescue in the Bristol Channel*, D. Bradford Barton, 1967; W. H. Mitchell & L. A. Sawyer, *The Empire Ships*, Lloyds of London Press, 1990; W. H. Jones, *History of the Port of Swansea*, W. Spurrell & Sons, 1922; W. B. Hallam, *Blow Five: A History of the Alexandra Towing Co. Ltd.*, J. O. C. Publications, 1976; *Lloyds War Losses (Vol 1)*; Basil Greenhill, *The Merchant Schooners; The Story of the Kathleen & May* (published by *Ships Monthly* in Association with The Maritime Trust), Endlebury Publishing Co., 1972; Nicholas T. Cairis, *Passenger Liners of the World since 1893*, Bonanza Books, 1979; Frank O. Braynard & William H. Miller, *Fifty Famous*

Liners, Patrick Stevens, 1987; H. T. Lenton & J. J. Colledge, *Warships of World War II*, Ian Allan, 1964; *Lloyds Registers of Shipping; Sea Breezes; Ships Monthly;* E. C. Talbot-Booth, *Merchant Ships*, Sampson Low, Marstons Co., 1937; Norman L. Middlemiss, *Pride of the Princes*, Shield Publications, 1988, and *The British Tankers*, Shield Publications, 1989; J. Beynon, *An Eye-Witness Account of Shipwrecks on the Gower Coast . . .;* C. R. Vernon Gibbs, *British Passenger Liners of the Five Oceans*, Putnam, 1963; Patrick Beaver, *Yes, We Have Some . . . The Story of Fyffes*, P. C. Publications, 1976; H. M. Le Fleming, *Ships of the Blue Funnel Line*, Adlard Coles, 1961; John Anderson, *Last Survivors in Sail*, Percival Marshall & Co., 1948; George Musk, *A Short History and Fleet List of the Canadian Pacific Ocean Steamships, 1891-1961*, Canadian Pacific Railway, London, n.d.; Tony Atkinson & Kevin O'Donoghue, *Blue Star*, World Ship Society, 1985; *Marine News; Central Record; The Cambrian; Cambrian Daily Leader; South Wales Daily Post; South Wales Evening Post; Herald of Wales; Western Mail.*

Finally, my sincere thanks to my parents for their support, and to Lilian Joyce Dhar for reading endless hand-written and typed articles, and for proof reading the book.

Foreword

From the day it first appeared in the *South Wales Evening Post* in 1985 'On the Waterfront' was bound to be a huge success. For those thousands of our readers who lived and worked in the shadow of the busy port it awoke old memories. And it sparked the imagination of those who were too young to remember.

Every week Gareth Mills's words and pictures sailed into our columns—and before our readers' very eyes the magnificent liners, tough cargo ships, battered tugs, brave warships and the men who crewed them, lived again in the pages of the *Evening Post.*

Few items from the busy columns of an evening newspaper can successfully be captured between the covers of a book.

Happily, however, I think readers of this volume will agree that 'On the Waterfront' has lost nothing in the translation from the immediacy of newsprint to the more lasting pages of a book. We were delighted to give Gareth Mills space in the *Evening Post* and are very pleased to see his hard work collected in this volume. We know it will bring many memories, happy and sad, flooding back. It is a tribute to Gareth's dedication and the bravery and skill of all those who feature in his writing.

Nick Carter,
Editor, *South Wales Evening Post,*
1987-1993

Introduction

Since the earliest days of sail, the many inlets and anchorages along the coast of south-west Wales have provided a safe haven for a host of ships. Those first harbours were set to become important coastal trading centres and, with the expansion of overseas trade, several of them were to grow into major commercial ports handling a multiplicity of cargoes. Over the centuries, a vast tide of imports and exports have been handled by the ports and harbours ranged along this coastline. Though the tide of trade is now on the ebb, the people of south-west Wales retain a deep love of the sea and a fondness for the ships which have carried British goods to all corners of the globe.

'On the Waterfront', the weekly series which appeared in the *South Wales Evening Post*, Swansea, between November 1985 and December 1991, told many of those stories concerning the tramps, tankers, tenders and tugs, ore carriers, container ships and cruise liners which found haven in the Port of Swansea and neighbouring harbours. During those six years it provided for thousands of readers a reminder of the debt we owe our merchant marine and to those who strive to keep our vital trade routes open both in times of peace and war.

The series has reached out as far as New Zealand, Canada and the United States and has served to bring about more than one reunion. In 1941 the lives of two Swansea men touched as a wartime drama unfolded around them in the Atlantic. They were not to meet again until, years later, they read an account of the incident in 'On the Waterfront'. Both wrote to the *Evening Post* who put them back in touch.

A broad range of subjects has been covered, from a radio-controlled model aircraft flight over Swansea's South Dock to the arrival at Port Talbot of an iron ore carrier with one of the largest recorded deadweights and an overall length greater than three rugby pitches. There have been tales told of drama on the high seas, shipwrecks, war exploits and human tragedy. The saddest, perhaps, concerned the first mate of the Norwegian vessel *Helvetia* wrecked near the tip of the Gower peninsula in a storm in 1887. He was given lodgings at a house in the village and fell in love with the family's eldest daughter, who returned his love. When he was leaving for home he sought her father's permission to write to her. He was refused. What became of him isn't known. But the girl he loved remained true to him. She died, unmarried, in her eighties.

'On the Waterfront' recorded some 310 stories in all, drawn from Milford Haven in the west to Newport in the east, and over 100 of these are retold in this amply illustrated book.

Gareth A. Mills

The aftermath of the 1865 disaster.

It was at approximately 6.30 a.m. on 29 November 1865 that disaster struck at the pontoon bridge which carried the Vale of Neath Railway over the North Dock at Swansea.

The bridge, worked by hydraulic power, could be opened and closed in a short space of time. Normally, it was left open one and a half hours before and about three hours after high water, so that the river traffic was not impeded.

A heavy coal train of 32 broad-gauge trucks, each containing about 300 tons of coal, and drawn by one of the best and most powerful engines of the Vale of Neath Railway Company was ready to proceed to the South Dock from the Eastern coal depot. The usual precautions were taken to make certain that the line was clear, and the bridges closed.

The signalmen at both bridges gave the signal —'line clear'. For some inexplicable reason, however, the signalman at the bridge over the North Dock gave the 'all right' signal by telegraph although the bridge was not at the time closed. The signal having being received, the train was ordered to start her journey. Regrettably, the mechanical danger signal, worked by the bridge itself, could not have been seen by the engine driver or fireman, for the engine, trucks and their contents plunged into the dock lock. The driver and fireman were killed.

1

Seamark on station at Swansea.

Beaufort in Swansea Bay.

Wearing her new colours, a sunburst-yellow hull with a broad band of cardinal red, and white superstructure—a colour scheme adopted to make her distinctive at sea—*Seamark* was commissioned on 8 December 1959 as she lay berthed in the South Dock Basin, Swansea. The commissioning service which took place on the deck of the Swansea Pilotage Authorities' new cutter was conducted by the Bishop of Swansea and Brecon, Dr. J. J. A. Thomas; Canon H. C. Williams, Vicar of Swansea; the Rev. A. T. M. Jasper, Chaplain to the Mission to Seamen, and the Rev. R. Roberts, Chaplain to the Swansea Sailors Society.

Seamark was the latest addition in a long line of famous Swansea cutters. The earlier vessels were sailing craft and those in use in the second half of the eighteenth century were unique. Their distinctive rig—a vertical foremast and a raked main mast—could not be seen along any other section of the British coast.

It was in 1898 when Swansea pilots turned to steam-driven cutters, and the *Beaufort*, the first of the new era, made history. She was the first steam-driven pilot cutter in the world to be built for the purpose of laying alongside vessels at sea, thereby allowing pilots to embark and disembark directly. This practice, established at Swansea when pilotage first began, has been continued ever since.

Specially built for her job by P. K. Harris (Shipbuilders) Ltd., Appledore, the *Seamark* has a length of 112 feet, a beam of 23ft. 3ins., and a draught of 8ft. 6ins. Her two 480 bhp (brake horse power) engines, geared to a single shaft, give her a speed of 12 knots. The vessel remains in service.

The wreck of the *Duisberg*.

The *Duisberg* was a fine three-masted wooden barque of 997 gross tons, built in 1856 by J. Lanage, Vegesack for her owners Westergaard & Company, Christiana. She had a length of 183ft., a beam of 35ft. and a draught of 21ft.

During the winter of 1899 the Norwegian vessel, under the command of Captain Olsen, was sailing from Canada to Swansea laden with timber. Sixty days had been allowed for the journey but during the course of the voyage the ship encountered severe weather.

When off the banks of Newfoundland, the vessel sprung a leak. The captain endeavoured to put in at the Azores but, owing to adverse winds, failed to do so. He also tried to make for a harbour in Ireland, but again failed. By now the pumps had been going incessantly for nearly sixty days.

As the *Duisberg* approached Lundy Island a strong wind was blowing, waves were breaking over the vessel, and she was in danger of going under. Near Oxwich Point the captain tried to put out the anchors, but this proved impossible. People on the shore thought the barque had been abandoned, because as the vessel came nearer they could see that she was drifting up-channel broadside on.

The *Duisberg* eventually struck the rocks bow-on, on the west side of Oxwich Point on Saturday, 11 November 1899. The captain and crew made for the shore in the ship's lifeboat, taking with them as much of the boat's effects as they could handle. But no sooner had they left the side of the vessel the *Duisberg* started to break, the fore and main masts crashing down. The captain and crew found it difficult to land but, guided by coastguards, they managed to beach the lifeboat safely on the sands near Oxwich Church.

As soon as Miss Talbot heard of the disaster she expressed her deep concern for the men by giving a donation of five shillings to each member of the crew.

On 27 November 1899 Mr. Evan Crapper sold by public auction at Oxwich Point the hull, masts, rigging and cabin furniture of the *Duisberg*, whilst the vessel itself, which was deemed a total wreck, was sold to a Mr. Thomas of Oxwich Green, for £33.10s., on condition that she should be left undisturbed until the whole of the cargo was discharged. Her cargo consisted of spruce, deal and birch boards, which were made into rafts, launched into the sea and towed away.

Beaching the *Lochgoil* off Mumbles, with tugs in attendance, 7 October 1939.

The *Marwarri* beached at Mumbles, 1939.

Mumbles Lifeboat Station had a busy period during the early years of the Second World War. The first launch took place on 6 October 1939, when the reserve lifeboat *J. B. Proudfoot* landed 45 persons from the 9,462 gross ton Royal Mail vessel *Lochgoil*.

The *Lochgoil* was bound for Vancouver from Newport when she struck a mine about five miles from the *Scarweather* light vessel. The crew had been taken off by the Cardiff vessel *Philipp M*, which was subsequently escorted to Mumbles by the lifeboat. At Mumbles the crew were ferried ashore and the injured were conveyed in Red Cross vehicles to hospital.

The *Lochgoil* was grounded off Mumbles in order to lighten the vessel and to salvage as much of the cargo as possible. She was later brought into the port and docked at Palmers Dry Dock.

In 1940 she was renamed *Empire Rowan* but three years later, on 27 March 1943, she was sunk by an aircraft torpedo in the Bay of Collo, north-west of Bone, Algeria.

The *Lochgoil* was built by Harland and Wolff, of Glasgow, in 1922 for Royal Mail Lines Ltd.

The *Marwarri*, owned by Thos and Jno Brocklebank Ltd, Liverpool, had the doubtful distinction of being one of the first magnetic-mine casualties shortly after the outbreak of the Second World War.

The vessel was on a passage from Belfast to Newport, where she had been loading anti-aircraft stores. On 5 October 1939, a few miles south of the *Scarweather* lightship, she was rocked by a violent explosion. Believing his ship had been torpedoed, the master ordered all boats into the water and made his way over to the light-vessel to request that a signal be sent calling for tug assistance. All the crew survived, and only six needed hospital treatment.

The *Marwarri* was later beached at Mumbles and ten days later was pumped dry and towed into dry dock at Swansea. It seems that the mine explosion had lifted and violently shaken the ship for, although there was no hole in the hull, all cast iron fittings had shattered, and fractures had allowed water to enter the holds.

After the vessel had been made seaworthy, the *Marwarri* went on to play an important role as a D-Day transport ship and came through the rest of the war unscathed. In 1963 she was sold to Hong Kong breakers.

The *Empire Daughter* loading coal at Port Talbot docks in 1945.

Like other ports in the United Kingdom, Swansea had lost several ships during the last war, but with victory in Europe, the thoughts of Swansea ship-owners were turning to the problem of replacements.

One such loss took place on 13 September 1941 when the Swansea collier *Bloomfield*, of 1,417 gross tons, built in 1920 by G. Brown & Co., Greenock and owned by Harries Bros., Swansea was bombed and sunk off the Faroe Islands by a German aircraft. Her master was Captain W. J. Bie, a familiar figure at Swansea docks, who got his crew away without losing a man. His vessel, however, suffered the same fate of another of the company's ships, the *Amiens* (1,548 gross tons), which had been sunk off Trevose Head, Cornwall, on 16 April the same year.

In August 1945, however, Messrs Harries Bros. and Company of Swansea received confirmation from the War Office and Ministry of Transport that two practically new colliers, the *Empire Daughter* and *Empire Peggotty*, both of 2,066 gross tons and built in 1944, had been allocated to them under the Tonnage Replacement Scheme. Both vessels were registered at Swansea. The *Empire Daughter*, a vessel of the most modern type, was put under the command of Captain Bie. A self-trimming collier with large hatches strengthened to withstand the stress of heavy seas, the *Empire Daughter*—like the *Empire Peggotty*—was designed to operate the near continental trade on which south Wales relied so much in pre-war days.

Another note of progress was struck in the crew's accommodation. Instead of living in the forecastle of ancient but unhappy memory, they were accommodated amidships and enjoyed the almost complete privacy of only two bunks to a berth. The ship's owners also installed a wireless set in each department for entertainment purposes. In addition, there were eight shower berths for refreshing after coaling.

In 1946, the *Empire Daughter* was resold to Harries Bros. and renamed *Glanrhyd*. In 1949, she became the *Noeldale* for the Tavistock Supply Company, London. In 1961 the vessel was sold to Henry and McGregor and rechristened *Kinnaird Head*, and renamed *Brick Quinto* in the following year. The ship was sold for breaking-up in Italy in 1976.

The *Helvetia*, 1887: a fine drawing by James Harris jnr (kindly loaned by Mrs. J. M. Thomas).

Mumbles, although sheltered to some extent by its towering hill, felt the full fury of a storm which passed over Swansea on Monday, 31 October and Tuesday, 1 November 1887. Various craft were eagerly watched from the shore by the fishermen, who were ready to launch the lifeboat and go to their aid, if needed.

At Caswell Bay the American windmill, which had been erected by the Waterworks Company (and was shortly to be opened by Lady John Jones Jenkins of The Grange, Westcross), was blown down. The mill was to replace steam as the motive power used to pump water from the well in the Caswell rocks, which was the main source of supply for the Mumbles.

The Norwegian barque *Helvetia* drifted ashore near the Worm's Head on Tuesday, 1 November 1887, and became a total wreck. On the Monday evening Captain Stevenson reported that he was off the Mumbles, burning flare-up lights and other signals in the vain hope of attracting the attention of a pilot. By 8.00a.m. on the Tuesday morning the vessel was seen standing down-channel abreast of the Helwick Buoy, at which time the wind was blowing a strong gale and backing south-west. The *Helvetia* was labouring very heavily and drifting to leeward. Eventually, she drifted across the Helwick Shoal, losing part of her deck cargo in the process, and then ran round the Worm's Head into Rhosili Bay where she let go her anchors. While at anchor near the Worm's Head she struck the rocks.

The coastguard and the rocket brigade stationed at Rhosili got their apparatus across the sound and on to the Worm's Head. Communication was established with the vessel and one man was brought ashore. The remaining crew members refused to leave their vessel but, as the tide rose, they too decided to come ashore, together with effects, in their boats, leaving the *Helvetia* riding at anchor under the shelter of Worm's Head. At 5.30p.m., however, she parted from her anchor and was driven on to the sands, where her remains still lie. Her 500 tons of wood was discharged on the beach and every available man, horse and cart was employed for weeks gathering the cargo together. Subsequently the wood was purchased by south Wales timber merchants, who arranged for ships to take the timber away during the summer. It was said that the *Helvetia* brought more money to the neighbourhood than any other wreck.

There is also an interesting postscript relating to the wreck of the *Helvetia*. The captain and the mate were lodged in the village for a few weeks after their ship had been wrecked. At the house where the first mate was staying, his host had five daughters, the eldest about 20 years of age. The mate fell in love with her and she with him. On leaving for home, the young man asked the father's permission to write to his eldest daughter—but this was refused. It is not known what became of him, but the lady remained single until her dying day.

This composite photograph of the King's Dock, Swansea was taken in 1951. From right to left, the 8,523 gross ton *South Africa Star* is loading tin and general cargo at D Shed for Australia. Launched by the Seattle-based Tacoma Shipping Corporation in 1943 as an escort carrier for the U.S. Navy, she was purchased by Blue Star Line in 1948 and converted to a cargo liner. In 1967 she was sold to Japan for demolition.

At No. 3 Quay (centre), is the twin screw motor vessel (m.v.) *Clan Macdonald*, 8,150 gross ton, which is also loading tin and general cargo for Australia. Built at Greenock Dockyard in 1939 for the Clan Line, she was sold by the Houston Line to Chinese mainland shipbreakers, and arrived at Shanghai in August, 1970.

At C Shed, the 3,575 gross ton *Memphis* is loading general cargo for one of the Mediterranean ports. The *Memphis* was built in 1947 by Wm. Pickersgill and Sons Ltd., Sunderland, and owned by Moss Hutchinson. During 1972, she was sold to Sifmonau Shipping Co., Greece, and renamed *Elias*. There she remained until 1981 when she was sold to Pakistani shipbreakers.

On the extreme left of the picture is the steam tug *Benson*, owned by Alexandra Towing Co. Ltd. Built in 1908 by J. Cran & Co., Leith, she was sold to the Admirality on completion. Purchased by Dewsbury, Swansea, in 1924, she was renamed *Benson*. The towing interests of Dewsbury's were taken over by Alexandra Towing Co., and with them the *Benson*. The vessel ceased service at Port Talbot docks in August 1960, and was laid up. The *Benson* left the port on 14 October 1960, destined to be broken-up at West Cork.

Detail of the damage caused to the deck and side of the tanker *Olav Ringdal Jr.* by the explosion.

A huge explosion woke many thousands of the residents of Swansea shortly after 4.30a.m. on 27 November 1954 as a blast ripped through the Norwegian oil tanker *Olav Ringdal Jr.,* owned by Olav Ringdals Tankrederi A/S, Oslo. The 9,829 gross ton tanker had been moored at the east lay-by in the Queen's Dock after discharging her cargo of oil from Hena-Al-Ahmadi. The explosion occurred near the engine room, and despite the efforts of the firemen, flames from the engine-room structure shot high into the air for a period of two hours. Most of the crew of forty-two were able to leave the vessel in orderly fashion, but many jumped overboard and clung to rafts and pieces of wood before being picked up by Swansea boatmen. Others were found swimming or clinging to ropes at the side of the tanker. Sadly, three crewmen died, and twelve were injured in the blast and fire. However, twelve Swansea men, employed by T. Crimes & Co. Ltd, the Swansea

boiler scalers, who were aboard the tanker at the time, all escaped uninjured.

As dawn broke a thick pull of smoke hung over the Queen's Dock and the glow of the flames could be seen for a considerable distance. The light of day also revealed how near the tanker was to other vessels in the dock. The forward section of the *Olav Ringdal Jr.* was more or less untouched, the green and white paint looking neat and new, but the entire aft portion of the vessel was seared and blackened by the heat. Lifeboats, in their davits, were splintered by the force of the explosion, and where the ship was almost broken in two, huge steel plates were folded and twisted like pieces of paper.

It was necessary to part the bow and stern sections using oxyacetylene cutters and explosives, after which the forward section was towed to Liverpool by the tug *Turmoil*. The after section left Swansea under the tow of the tugs *Oostzee* and *Poolzee*.

A fine shot of the steam tug *Canning* (left), under the command of Captain Phil Grimshaw, and *Crosby* (right) manouvering the 4,978 gross ton *City of Dundee* in the King's Dock, Swansea, in 1966.

Canning, now a floating exhibit lying alongside Swansea's Industrial and Maritime Museum, was built in 1954 by Cochrane and Sons Ltd, of Selby for the Alexandra Towing Company and worked in Liverpool before coming to Swansea in 1965. Of 200 tons and 1,000 ship horse power, she was sold to the city council in 1975.

The *Crosby*, of 215 tons and similar horsepower to *Canning*, was built in 1937. She took part in salvage operations when the submarine *Thetis* went down in Liverpool Bay in 1939. She worked in Swansea from 1966 to 1967 and was broken up the following year at Dalmuir.

The *City of Dundee* was built in 1961 for the Ellerman and Bucknall Steam Ship Co. Ltd. Although renamed *Dundee* in 1978 the vessel was rechristened the *City of Dundee* two years later. The ship was scrapped in Pakistan in 1984.

The *Roche Castle* wrecked and pounded by heavy seas below Paviland Cliff, Gower. The wreck was photographed by local photographer D. G. Holman, whose striking images appeared in papers around the world.

The most prestigious wreck-service award for 1937 went to the Rhosili Life Saving Company— the first time the Board of Trade's shield had come to Wales. Behind the award lies an epic story of the rescue of all but one of the eleven-strong crew of the trawler *Roche Castle*, which struck the rocks on a rough and foggy night in 1937.

About 9.30p.m. on Sunday, 10 January one of Consolidated Fisheries' trawlers, the *Roche Castle*, was returning from the fishing grounds off the south-west coast of Ireland with the intention of docking on Monday morning, when she ran ashore about twelve miles west of Mumbles and radioed that assistance was required immediately.

A search of the coast was at once organised and the vessel located under Paviland cliffs, on the south coast of the Gower peninsula. The Mumbles Lifeboat was launched and the Rhosili Life Saving Company made its way to the scene. It seemed for a time that there was little hope for the trawler's crew when the lorry carrying the Rhosili company's men and equipment became stuck in the mud a mile from the wreck. However, the gear was manhandled with great difficulty over the cliff to a position about a hundred yards from the vessel.

Communication with the trawler was established with the second rocket fired, and the whip sent out. A hawser was later hauled aboard the vessel and secured.

Had the crew come ashore at that stage the rescue would have been successful, but they signalled their intention to stay aboard in an effort to save the ship.

By the early hours of Monday morning, 11 January, the seas were breaking over the vessel and the crew, realising conditions were now desperate, attempted to come ashore. The first two men got into the breeches buoy, but as they were being hauled-in the vessel gave a heavy lurch which resulted in one man being catapulted into the air before falling and drowning in the boiling surf. His companion was hauled ashore, followed by the remaining ten crew members in the space of three-quarters of an hour. A remarkable feat.

Members of the Rhosili Life Saving Company had worked magnificently under the most appalling conditions, and in recognition of the men's leadership and courage in carrying out the rescue during the hours of darkness, the Board of Trade awarded the district officers a silver bowl.

The *Protesilaus* broken in two, February 1940.

The fore-part of the *Protesilaus* being beached off Mumbles, February 1940.

September 1939 will always be remembered as the month that Britain declared war on Germany. And within a few hours of the declaration the liner *Athenia*, belonging to the Donaldson Line, was torpedoed off Scotland. On 12 September one of the first vessels to come into contact with a magnetic mine was beached at Mumbles.

By now the Germans had been busy in the English Channel, and had been laying magnetic mines around the British coast. Many ships came to grief, and the lifeboats and their crews were called upon to perform heroic rescues. Two such rescues were performed within three weeks of one another during 1940.

The first was on the morning of 21 January 1940. The Mumbles Lifeboat was launched and in very cold and damp weather found the 9,577 gross ton *Protesilaus* of Liverpool which had struck a mine six miles south-west of Mumbles Head.

The *Protesilaus* was inward-bound light, when there was a terrific explosion. The vessel had struck a mine and was severely holed about midships. All those aboard were ordered to the boat stations and all sixty crew members, including a canary found alive in its cage, got away from the ship listing ominously to port. After having initially been taken aboard a tanker the crew, with the exception of thirteen injured men, were subsequently transferred to a naval vessel which took them to port. The injured men were placed on board the Mumbles Lifeboat, *Edward, Prince of Wales*, and on landing taken to hospital.

The fifth engineer, Mr. P. Freeman, of London, had a lucky but uncomfortable escape. He was in his cabin when the explosion occurred but was blown out of the room by the blast. Outside he found it bitterly cold dressed only in singlet and trousers, and one shoe! The gunner also had a narrow escape when the magazine on board exploded.

The *Protesilaus* was the first casualty of the Blue Funnel fleet and a few weeks after she was mined, she was towed into Mumbles and beached off West Cross, where she broke in two. The vessel was found to be beyond economical repair. The stern section was transported to Thos. W. Ward Ltd, Briton Ferry, on 11 July 1940 for breaking up. The fore section was also towed to Briton Ferry but in August it arrived in tow at Greenock for use as a block ship at Scapa Flow.

The *Protesilaus* was built by Hawthorn Leslie & Co., Newcastle, and completed in 1910. She was owned by the China Mutual Steam Navigation Co. Ltd (Alfred Holt Managers).

The general cargo trader *Cato* being towed into Swansea by the steam tugs *Waterloo* and *Clyneforth*.

Still flying the regulation 'Not under command' signal, the general cargo trader *Cato* was brought into Swansea by the steam tugs *Waterloo* and *Clyneforth* during March 1962 after spending a night at sea in a gale-force wind.

The 945 gross ton m.v. *Cato* was owned by the Bristol Steam Navigation Co. Ltd, and was on passage in ballast from Newport to Swansea. Near Nash Point her engines failed and when she dropped her two anchors they failed to hold. Although the *Cato* sustained no damage the vessel gradually drifted helplessly towards the Scarweather lightship, a distance of more than ten miles. She had company for part of the time as the *Echo*, another of the company's vessels, was on passage from Cardiff to Swansea.

The *Echo* stood by the *Cato* for most of the night and early morning until the *Clyneforth*, owned by the Britannia Steam Towing Company of Swansea, arrived on the scene in response to an urgent call.

The *Clyneforth*, commanded by Captain T. A. Pickard, was later joined by the steam tug *Waterloo*, owned by the Alexandra Towing Company. Under the command of Captain B. Byrne, the two tugs brought the helpless vessel into port. With the wind almost gale force and the *Cato* helpless, it was not an easy operation and for

a considerable time there was doubt as to whether the vessels could make port on the morning tide, with the tug *Waterloo* ahead and the *Clyneforth* astern.

Captain Walter Keys, master of the *Cato*, was still on his bridge when the vessel finally docked. 'It was just bad luck that our engines should fail in such weather,' he said.

A member of the crew of the *Echo*, which docked at Swansea some hours before the *Cato*, said the weather conditions were particularly bad. 'The seas were very high,' he commented, 'and the wind did not let up for a second.'

The *Cato* also came to a sad end. On 24 April 1963 it sank at Avonmouth Docks after it had been struck by the Ellerman Lines' *City of Brooklyn* (7,557 gross tons). The ship was raised on 26 May 1963, but it was a total loss. She was sold to John Cashmore Ltd, Newport, for breaking-up following her arrival at the port on 13 June 1963.

The *Cato* was built by the Goole Shipbuilding & Repairing Co. Ltd, and completed in June 1946.

The tug *Waterloo* was sold in 1972 to Italian owners and renamed *Dritto*. During 1989 she was sold for breaking-up. The *Clyneforth* was sold in 1966 to Piraeus under the name of *Ena* following her acquisition by the Greek owners.

The *Manzanares* berthed at King's Dock, Swansea, 1932.

It was in 1931 that Elders and Fyffes established a port in Swansea for all its vessels engaged in the continental trade. Fyffes' vessels were very attractive in appearance, with their pale creamy-buff funnels and their silver-grey hulls, which looked almost white in the sunlight. The ships were given Spanish or South American place-names.

The photograph shows s.s. *Manzanares* berthed at B Shed, King's Dock, Swansea, in 1932. The 4,061 gross ton vessel was built by Alex Stephen and Sons, Glasgow in 1911. She had a service speed of 13½ knots and accommodation for a few passengers. In 1939, four years after she was sold to Union Handels, Germany, and renamed *Vegesack* she was wrecked near Stavanger, Norway. Ironically, her sister ship, the *Aracataca* had been victorious in a single-handed battle with a German submarine in March 1917. Later that year, however, she collided with the s.s. *Moliere* and was lost off Beachy Head.

The stern of the vessel ahead of the *Manzanares* is believed to be that of the s.s. *Calchas*, built in 1921 by Workman, Clark & Co., Belfast, for Alfred Holt & Co.

14

Ex HMS *Bermuda* berthed at Briton Ferry, 1965.

The River Neath was the scene of another last berthing when the 8,000 gross ton HMS *Bermuda*, arrived at the graveyard of ships at Briton Ferry. This once proud fighting ship is pictured awaiting the oxyacetylene burners and breakers' hammers.

Bermuda was built by John Brown and Co. Ltd, Clydebank, launched on 11 September 1941 and completed on 5 August 1942. She was armed with nine six-inch guns, eight four-inch anti-aircraft guns and six 21-inch torpedo tubes. The ship had a speed of 31 knots. During the Second World War the *Bermuda* saw service off North Africa, in the Atlantic and in the Arctic. HMS *Bermuda* arrived in Swansea Bay on 26 August 1965 from Portsmouth under the tow of the naval tug *Bustler*. She was subsequently towed by three Swansea-based tugs as far as Ferry Boat wharf where her mast was cut down so that she could pass under the River Neath road bridge to Thos. W. Ward Ltd. As *Bermuda* was being manoeuvered across Swansea Bay the following message was signalled by the cruiser to the anti-aircraft frigate HMS *Puma* which was making her first visit to the Port of Swansea: 'We who are about to die salute you'.

The *Minnedosa* at the Queen Alexandra Dock, Cardiff, 1929.

The Canadian-Pacific Railway Company's liner s.s. *Minnedosa*, 15,186 gross tons, is pictured arriving at the Queen Alexandra Dock, Cardiff, on 25 May 1929, where she was greeted by Canadian Pacific officials, and relatives and friends of the nearly 300 Welsh emigrants who were due to embark for Canada and the United States.

The emigrants, and friends, who had come to wish them *bon voyage* and good luck in their new life as Empire settlers, were transported in special trains from Cardiff Central Station to the quayside, where the *Minnedosa* was berthed. In addition to the Welsh emigrants, the liner also carried mail.

The *Minnedosa* was launched by Barclay Curle and Co. Ltd, in October 1917, and arrived in tow for completion by Harland and Wolff Ltd, Belfast, in May 1918. During November 1918 she was delivered for service as a troopship and the following month she sailed on her first Canadian-Pacific voyage from Liverpool.

In 1935, the *Minnedosa* was sold to Ricuperi Metallici of Turin, for breaking-up, but was bought by the Italian Line for service as a troopship and renamed *Piemonte*. During August 1943, she was scuttled at Messina, salvaged in 1949 and left in tow for Spezia for breaking-up.

The *George Washington* arrives at the lock to the Queen Alexandra Dock, Cardiff, on Sunday, 29 July 1928. At the time she was probably the largest liner ever to enter the Bristol Channel, and the Cardiff-bound passengers included 500 Welsh-Americans. The vessel, under the command of Captain Randall, was regarded as one of the most luxurious ships on the Atlantic service, and enjoyed an established reputation among ocean travellers. With a length of 700ft, the 23,788 gross ton *George Washington* had accommodation for 2,923 passengers divided into four classes, and a speed of 18 knots. Built by A. G. Vulcan, Stettin, Germany, for the North German Lloyd line in June 1909, she was laid up at New York during the First World War until the United States entered the war. The vessel was then acquired by the United States Government and converted into a troopship.

In 1920 the ship was taken over by the U.S. Mail Company. A year later, following the collapse of the company, the vessel was handed over to the United States Lines. At the beginning of the Second World War the *George Washington* was acquired by the British government, converted during 1940 into a troopship, and renamed *Catlin*. She returned to the United States in 1941 and recovered her original name. With one of her funnels removed, and converted to oil burning, she was once again used for trooping until decommissioned in 1947, and laid up. The ship was sold for scrap in 1951 after being destroyed by fire at Baltimore.

The *Deucalion* berthed at King's Dock, Swansea, 1970.

A ship with a most distinguished war record paid her first visit to Swansea Docks in October, 1970. She was the m.v. *Deucalion* (ex-*Glengyle*), of the Glen Line, which loaded a cargo of tinplate, steel sheet and scrap at the King's Dock for the Far East.

At the outbreak of the Second World War the Admiralty had taken a keen interest in the *Glengyle* and *Denbighshire* because of their high speed, and they were soon requisitioned, along with the *Breconshire*, and converted into fleet-supply ships for service under the White Ensign.

In 1940 the *Glengyle* was converted and commissioned as an infantry landing ship. In February 1941 she formed part of Force Z and sailed to the Mediterranean, carrying out a raid on Bardia. In April she took part in Operation Demon, the evacuation of Greece, and in May landed a battalion of troops in Crete. In June the vessel formed part of Operation Exporter, landing troops in Syria. The following January the *Glengyle* was part of Convoy MF2, destined for Malta, and Convoy ME9, from Malta to Alexandria, returning to the United Kingdom in April. In November she was present during Operation Torch, the invasion of North Africa.

In July 1943, the *Glengyle* took part in Operation Husky, the invasion of Sicily, and in the same month formed part of Convoy MEF36 from Malta to Egypt, flying the broad pennant of Commodore of Convoy. August and September operations included voyages between Egypt, Tripoli, Algiers and Malta. On 7 October, she hoisted the flag of Naval Commander, Force A, and proceeded in convoy to Bombay. In December the vessel formed part of Force G and returned to the Mediterranean.

On 19 January 1944, she took part in Operation Shingle, the landing at Anzio, and in May transported naval units to Corsica. Following refits at Liverpool in June 1944 and April 1945 she sailed in July 1945 for India, via the Mediterranean, and in August took part in Operation Armour, the transport of No. 3 Commando Brigade and 132 RAF Spitfire Squadron to Hong Kong. In September she evacuated 600 interned Britons from Hong Kong to Madras.

In March 1970 the 9,800 gross ton *Glengyle* was transferred to the Ocean Steamship Co. and renamed *Deucalion*. She was finally sold to Taiwanese ship-breakers, arriving at Kaohsiung on 9 June 1971.

The coal trimmers: (left to right) Edward Bradley, Ronnie Russell, Alf Young, Charles Quick and William Cassell.

Five of the coal trimmers and tippers who had to run for their lives as 30 loaded coal trucks careered out of control towards a coal hoist at King's Dock, Swansea, in June, 1967.

Two of the trucks tipped over the edge and lodged between No. 11 hoist and the 1,795 gross ton French steamship *Psyche,* which had been loading 2,300 tons of coal. Miraculously no one was hurt, but loading at the hoist stopped while dock engineers worked to remove the trucks. The wagons were each loaded with 15 tons of coal, and were waiting to be tipped when the wet and greasy rails sent them slithering forwards. 'There was no chance of stopping them,' a coal trimmer said later.

Apparently it all happened in a split second: there was a warning shout and everybody ran for their lives. Mr. Edward Bradley, the foreman in charge, and Mr. Alf Young narrowly escaped serious injury. They were under the coal shute but both managed to run to safety in the nick of time.

Seven tippers on the hoist also ran for cover as six wagons jack-knifed in the pile-up after the first two plunged over the edge.

19

The wedding group aboard the *Gladstone:* (left to right) Captain and Mrs Sverre Gramm; the bride and groom—Eldbjorg Olavson and Gunnar Raabe; Pastor A. B. Danielsen; Captain Brinley Byrne and members of his crew.

An unusual marriage took place at Swansea Docks during November 1949 when the Norwegian wireless operator on board the motor tanker *Pan Europe* in the Queen's Dock was married to a Norwegian typist on board the steam tug *Gladstone*, three-and-a-half miles south of Mumbles Head. The bridegroom was 22-year-old Gunnar Raabe, son of an Oslo travel-agency supervisor, and his bride was Eldbjorg Olavson, aged 21, daughter of Mr Sigurd Olavson, an Oslo schoolteacher.

The 9,468 gross ton *Pan Europe* arrived at Swansea on Sunday, 20 November but due to the

The steam tug *Gladstone* leaving port.

short time the vessel was expected to be in port arrangements had been made by the wireless officer for Gunnar Raabe's fiancée to join him at Swansea. She arrived on the Monday but because it was then too late to give the required three days' notice for the marriage licence, it was decided to charter the steam tug *Gladstone* from the Alexandra Towing Company Limited, and secure the services of Pastor A. B. Danielsen, of the Norwegian Church at Cardiff, to perform the service on board.

With the bridal couple, Captain Sverre Gramm of the *Pan Europe* and his wife Mrs Astrid Gramm, the Swansea Norwegian Church Pastor Oswald T. Bergstad, and an *Evening Post* reporter and photographer aboard, the *Gladstone* left the King's Dock about 9.00 a.m., heading due south after passing Mumbles Head. In accordance with Norwegian custom the bride was already wearing a plain ring which had been given to her on the occasion of the couple's engagement in 1947.

Two candles—provided by trimmers on board and placed in metal nuts—were burning during the delivery of Pastor Danielsen's sermon. After singing the Norwegian marriage hymn 'Love Comes from God', the small congregation made their way from the cabin to the tug's bridge where the pastor performed the marriage ceremony. Placing his hands on the head of both bride and groom kneeling before him, the pastor blessed the couple and said the Lord's Prayer. There followed the benediction and the ceremony was at an end.

The ceremony was officially recorded in the tug's log, signed by the couple and witnessed by the other Norwegians present.

Immediately after the ceremony, the *Gladstone* made her way back to Swansea Docks, where a reception was held on board the *Pan Europe* prior to leaving port that evening.

The *Pacific Star*, with tugs fore and aft, clears the mud bank on which the vessel grounded.

Speedy work by engineers at Swansea Docks and co-operation between tug owners and others averted serious delays to shipping during August 1956. On entering the King's Dock lock at midnight on 23 August the propellers of the 11,218 gross ton motor tanker *Pacific Star*, carrying a cargo of 15,400 tons of crude oil from Persia, fouled one of the wires operating the lock gates. In turn, a coping stone from the quay wall was pulled into the water fouling the lock so that the gate could not be closed behind the tanker.

In view of the possible danger arising from leaving a vessel with a cargo of oil in the lock, it was decided that the *Pacific Star* should return to her anchorage at Mumbles Roads. However, whilst making her way to sea again the tanker became grounded just off the end of the pier in the fairway leading to the dock entrance. Although some smaller vessels were able to make their way through the lock the *Pacific Star* remained firmly embedded, lying across the fairway.

On the morning of 29 August, ten tugs were gathered round the tanker ready to refloat her, while at the same time engineers of the British Transport Commission worked with a diver to remove the offending coping stone and satisfy themselves that the lock gate was still in working order. Almost miraculously, however, and in a matter of two or three minutes, the tanker moved away from the vicinity of the East Pier without the assistance of the waiting tugs. By this time the outer lock gates had also been opened, thereby facilitating the safe passage of all vessels.

The *Pacific Star* was built in January 1954 by Wm. Hamilton and Co. Ltd, Port Glasgow. Owned by Booth Steam Ship Company she was transferred to Blue Star ownership during 1961. Three years later the vessel was sold for £180,000 to Atlantic Overseas Bulk Carriers Inc. (Liberia) and renamed *Silver Bay*. In 1973 she was sold to Tung Ho Steel Enterprise Co. Ltd, and arrived at Kashsiung on 22 April 1973 for breaking-up.

The passenger liner *Inanda* being manoeuvred into Palmer's Dry Dock, Swansea, by the Alexandra Towing Company's steam tug *Wallasey*.

Swansea seemed more like a passenger port for ocean travellers in February 1932 as 49 passengers from the Harrison liner *Inanda* were landed at the King's Dock to enable the vessel to go into Palmer's Dry Dock for a new propeller blade. The mishap to the liner's propeller occurred on the Sunday evening, 31 January, when the *Inanda* was about 400 miles west of Land's End. The vessel put back to Falmouth slowly but on finding the dry dock occupied made her way to Swansea.

So efficient were the arrangements made by the owners and the local agents (Messrs. Burgess & Co. Ltd) that within fifteen minutes of berthing the vessel the passengers—most of whom were on a six-week cruise bound for Trinidad—were conveyed to the Hotel Metropole in a South Wales Transport bus.

Acting on behalf of the owners, the ships's local agents (Messrs. Burgess & Co.) arranged for the party to be taken on an excursion through the Gower peninsula in South Wales motor-buses. On their return they expressed their appreciation of the beautiful Gower coastline.

The 5,985 gross ton *Inanda* was built by Swan, Hunter & Wigham Richardson of Newcastle in 1925 especially for the passenger service between London and the West Indies. She had a speed of 13 knots and accommodation for 91 first-class passengers and a crew of 62.

On 7 September 1940, the *Inanda* was damaged and sunk in dock at London during a heavy bombing raid. Nevertheless she was raised and rebuilt by the Ministry of War Transport as a cargo vessel, and renamed *Empire Explorer*. On 9 July 1942, she was sunk by torpedo and gunfire from the U575 off Trinidad, West Indies.

The steam tug *Wallasey* was built in 1903 by J. T. Eltringham & Co., South Shields. In 1953 she was renamed *Cambrian* and six years later delivered to Thos. W. Ward Ltd, Briton Ferry for breaking-up.

A story of great courage and masterly seamanship unfolded during August 1931, with the arrival at Swansea of the Consolidated Fisheries steam trawler *Dunraven Castle*. It had on board the rescued members of the crew of the yacht *Maitenes II*, and in tow the craft itself which, despite the buffeting it had received in tempestuous seas off Land's End, appeared comparatively little damaged. The homecoming was marred only by the fact that out of the nine members of the yacht's crew, Colonel Hudson of Hull, a well-known trawler owner and part-owner of the yacht, had been washed overboard and lost when participating in the big race from Cowes to Land's End and Plymouth.

The circumstances which led to the tragedy were recalled by Lieutenant Luard, a retired naval officer and one of the yacht's crew. Quoting from the official log: 'They started on the Tuesday of August 11 in fairly good weather, but ran into a gale on the Thursday evening off Land's End and put into St Ives for shelter. On Friday morning they were under way by four o'clock. They rounded the Fastnet on Saturday at nine o'clock. The weather was steadily getting worse. The yacht was over-powered by terrific squalls and shipped heavy seas. At 11.45 on Sunday they lowered all sails, got the canvas off her and ran before the gale.'

At noon on Sunday Colonel Hudson, who was working aft, was lost overboard. Mountainous seas made it impossible for the crew to save him. The *Dunraven Castle* was sighted at 12.45 p.m. and was asked to stand by until the weather moderated. At 3.45p.m., however, the weather took a turn for the worse. But, despite the worsening conditions, those aboard the yacht and the vessel itself were eventually saved.

According to Lieutenant Luard, the manoeuvering of the *Dunraven Castle* was one of the finest pieces of seamanship he had ever seen. As the

The rescued yacht alongside the *Dunraven Castle* in the South Dock, Swansea, 1931.

trawler's boat, with four men aboard, went to put a line on the yacht their vessel was actually swept under the yacht. Nevertheless, the yacht was successfully boarded and they sailed her through the night with the trawler standing by. On the Monday morning the yacht was towed safely to Swansea by the trawler. Two of the men who made the hazardous attempt to reach the yacht in the ship's boat were W. Burgess, the bosun of Danygraig Road, St. Thomas, Swansea, and R. Reynolds, of Fern Street, Cwmbwrla, Swansea. Thanks to them and their colleagues and the clever manoeuvering of Captain Woods, of Birchwood, Mayhill Road, Swansea, eight yachtsmen were rescued.

The *City of Chelmsford*, owned by Ellerman & Bucknall Steam Ship Co. Ltd, is seen arriving at the Port of Swansea assisted by the steam tug *Brockenhurst* on her bow. To the left of the *City of Chelmsford* is the 8,314 gross ton tanker *Wave Ruler*, held fast on a sandbank outside the entrance to Swansea Docks in September 1953 after having been towed nearly 1,000 miles on becoming a 'dead ship' following the rupture of all her furnace boilers.

After one failed attempt to take her in tow, four tugs owned by Alexandra Towing Company, the *Langland, Benson, Neath* and *Alexandra,* went out on the evening tide, the *Langland* and *Neath* taking over forward, with the *Alexandra* and *Benson* aft. As the four tugs were bringing her in the *City of Chelmsford* became embedded and although all possible efforts were made to pull her clear the tanker remained firmly on the sandbank.

Further assistance was given by the Britannia Steam Towing Co. tugs *Kingforth* and *Majestic,* but the combined effort of the six tugs also failed to free the tanker.

The *Wave Ruler*, on charter to the Anglo-Iranian Oil Company, seemed to be held amidships and there appeared to be a pivot-like movement, but there was insufficient water to refloat her.

Fortunately, however, the position of the grounded tanker did not interfere with the incoming and outgoing traffic through the King's Dock lock gates. Indeed, two sister ships of the *Wave Ruler*, the *Wave Monarch* and *Wave Laird*, were already in port and both vessels played a part in lightening the cargo of the grounded oil tanker.

On Friday, 2 October, the *Wave Monarch*, having already taken 1,000 tons of crude oil on board, was again alongside in an effort to transfer a further 200-300 tons before high tide, when tugs would again attempt to move the *Wave Ruler* off the sandbank.

On the afternoon tide of Saturday, 3 October, five days after grounding, the *Wave Ruler* was finally refloated and taken into Swansea Docks. And after completing the discharge of her crude oil cargo, the *Wave Ruler* underwent repairs at Palmer's Dry Dock, Swansea.

The (ex *Empire Evesham*, 1947) *Wave Ruler* was built by Furness Shipbuilding Co. Ltd, Haverton Hill, and launched in January 1946. She was owned by the Admiralty. In 1976 she was sold 'as lies' for demolition and towed to Singapore. The vessel was finally broken-up in 1977.

The s.s. *Clan Stuart* is here pictured at the King's Dock, Swansea during the 1930s. It is being loaded with general cargo from the two-storey transit shed at the Mole, East End of the King's Dock, and was probably due to sail to India.

The 5,760 gross ton *Clan Stuart*, was built by Russell and Company Ltd of Port Glasgow in October 1916 for the Clan Line Steamers Limited (Cayzer, Irvine and Co. Ltd, Managers). On the night of 11 March 1940 she foundered off Start Point, Devon, following a collision with another vessel.

Also visible in the photograph is the stern section of the twin-screw motor ship *Peisander*, 6,225 gross tons, which, like the *Clan Stuart* is being loaded with general cargo. Built in 1925 by Caledon Ship Building and Engineering Company Ltd, Dundee for the Ocean Steam Ship Co. Limited (A. Holt and Company, Managers), this vessel had a rather small funnel at the after end of the superstructure. The *Peisander* was sunk by a U-boat off Nantucket on 17 May 1942.

The *Nevasa* making its way out into Swansea Bay. Alongside is the steam tug *Flying Kestrel* and the motor tug *Cambrian*.

Practically every secondary school in Carmarthenshire was represented when over 1,000 schoolchildren left Swansea Docks on Sunday, 4 June 1967 for a thirteen-day educational cruise to Madeira, Casablanca, Lisbon and Gibraltar. It took nearly two hours for the schoolchildren, aged between 12 and 15 years, to board the 20,527 gross ton *Nevasa* at the King's Dock for the first cruise of its kind to be arranged by the former Carmarthenshire Education Authority. The largest single party—114 girls—came from Llanelli, and the smallest, a party of ten from Llandybïe. The children were accompanied by 85 teachers and education authority staff. Also on board were 300 adults. The sailing of the *Nevasa* was probably the biggest passenger operation at the port since the last war.

During the voyage the *Nevasa* had to change course as a result of the outbreak of war in the Middle East. She was to have called at Casablanca but was diverted to Tenerife in the Canary Islands.

Originally built as a troopship in 1956 by Barclay, Curle and Co. Ltd, Glasgow, for the British India Steam Navigation Co. Ltd, the *Nevasa* was an ideal vessel for conversion to an educational cruise ship, a conversion carried out at Falmouth in 1965. After joining the P&O fleet as a cruise ship the *Nevasa* completed about 200 voyages, covering about three-quarters of a million miles, and carrying over 185,000 British and overseas schoolchildren. The vessel was eventually sold to Taiwan-based ship-breakers and it reached its final destination in March 1975.

Also making its way out into Swansea Bay with the *Nevasa* is the 244 gross ton steam tug *Flying Kestrel*, built in 1944 and broken-up at Passage West in 1969, and the 163 gross ton motor tug *Cambrian*, built in 1959. The latter vessel, renamed *Mari*, is believed to be in service to this day, working in the Grand Harbour, Valletta, Malta.

The tug *Mumbles* wrecked on Oxwich Point, 1931.

During thick fog and with a fairly heavy sea running, the Swansea tug *Mumbles* (owned by the British Tanker Company and in the charge of Captain Woodman of Gore Terrace, Swansea) went ashore on treacherous rocks in the west-facing corner of Oxwich Point, Gower, at 6.30a.m. on Wednesday, 25 February 1931. As the vessel appeared to be in danger of breaking up rapidly, the Mumbles lifeboat, *Edward, Prince of Wales* and the life-saving company based at Oxwich were called out and instructed to render any aid that might be necessary. In the meantime, however, the crew of seven men took to their own small boat and landed safely at Oxwich Bay, where they were provided with food and accommodation by Lady Blythswood.

Several attempts were made to refloat the vessel, but the assistance offered by the pilot cutter *Roger Beck*, the Mumbles lifeboat and an accompanying steam tug, and by the steam tug *Herculaneum*, owned by the Alexandra Towing Co., all proved in vain. Finally, in March 1931, after further energetic but unsuccessful attempts to prise the vessel off the rocks, it was decided to abandon all efforts to salvage the *Mumbles*. She eventually broke up. Ironically, the *Mumbles* was wrecked after having assisted another vessel in distress. Shortly after having been dry-docked, and a new propeller fitted, she had gone down channel to assist the disabled 6,891 gross ton tanker *British Motorist*. On returning up-channel in heavy fog and rolling seas she went ashore. The 195 gross ton, coal-burning tug, *Mumbles*, originally named *Marsden*, was built in 1917 by J. P. Reonnoldson Limited, South Shields.

The trawler *Barry Castle* in the South Dock, Swansea, 1949.

Just after midnight on Wednesday, 24 August 1949, after having been loaded with 60 tons of ice, the 380 ton trawler *Barry Castle* heeled over at her moorings at the ice wharf, South Dock, Swansea, and sank. As dawn broke only her superstructure and part of her prow were left above water, her port side and stern being completely submerged. However, efforts were soon made to prevent any further movement and arrangements were quickly in hand to right the vessel, built for the Admiralty by Cochrane & Sons Ltd, Selby in 1942 but later acquired by Consolidated Fisheries.

The *Barry Castle* was probably the first Swansea boat to fish in Icelandic waters. On 8 June she had returned to port with a catch which, allowing for the very bad weather experienced on the fishing grounds, was sufficient to encourage further excursions into North Atlantic waters. The 1,200 boxes—mainly cod and haddock of excellent quality—that were landed were regarded as 'not a bad start'. The trip, lasting 22 days, was undertaken after fitting out at Grimsby, the experiment having being undertaken because of the discouraging results obtained from fishing the 'home' grounds.

After lying on its port side in the South Dock Basin for seventeen days the steam trawler was finally placed in dry dock on Saturday, 10 September where she awaited examination before repair work began. The *Barry Castle* was raised by the 100 ton floating crane using two 6″ wire cables which were passed under the trawler from trunnions fastened to the starboard side. The salvage work was accomplished by the 500 ton salvage vessel *Ranger*, which saw service in both world wars but which achieved fame whilst salvaging the *Thetis* in Liverpool Bay in 1939.

The giant ore-carrier *Iron Bridge* at Port Talbot, 1987.

In October 1987 the *Iron Bridge* arrived at Port Talbot with one of the largest deadweights—173,000 tons—of any carrier to enter the harbour. The enormous bulk carrier, longer than three rugby pitches, subsequently discharged what was believed to be a record cargo, namely 134,500 tonnes of iron-ore pellet from Seven Islands, Canada.

The *Iron Bridge* is a sister ship of the *British Steel* which had 126,000 tonnes of cargo on board when she entered Port Talbot tidal harbour for the first time in July 1987.

The bulk carrier built by Harland and Wolff, Belfast, and launched in 1985, is owned by British Steel and managed by Furness Withy Ltd. Her dimensions are as follows: 945 feet long, 154 foot beam; and a maximum draught of 58 feet.

In the foreground is the motor tug *Alexandra*, 161 gross tons, which came into service with the Alexandra Towing Company at Swansea during May 1965. The vessel remains in service at Swansea.

The *Roland*, the ship that saved the lives of thirty men and women, berthed at King's Dock, Swansea, 1974.

The s.s. *Roland*, berthed at the King's Dock, Swansea whilst loading cargo for South America in October 1974. Earlier that year, the 7,322 gross ton cargo vessel carried out a dramatic rescue of the crew of a German vessel.

The *Roland*, under the command of Captain Bill Sparks, had called into the port of Santos, Brazil, after a long voyage from Liverpool. Later she stopped at Las Palmas for fresh water and then continued towards Rio de Janeiro. The vessel was steaming along at 15 knots, about 60 miles north of the equator, when the ship's radio officer asked Captain Sparks if they were anywhere near Saint Paul's rocks—a group of dangerous rocks around which swirled strong currents—for a Greek vessel had reported picking up an SOS signal from someone adrift in a lifeboat near the hazardous spot.

An hour later, Captain Sparks received more news. The people in distress were the crew of the 8,224 gross ton *Ana Cristina* on a voyage from Stockholm to Santos. On 26 March 1974 the vessel had struck an uncharted rock and sunk within ten minutes.

As the *Roland* was nearer to the SOS position than the Greek vessel, they proceeded to the location and by late afternoon had picked up signals from the Germans adrift in the lifeboats. All thirty-one crew members on board the two lifeboats were taken aboard the *Roland*. Amongst them were two women, a stewardess, and the wife of one of the crew. Within two days, the *Roland* put into the port of Recife, where the rescued crew were met by newspaper and television reporters.

The *Roland* was launched in 1950 as the *Dunedin Star* but was transferred in 1968 to the Lamport and Holt Line and renamed *Roland*. She was renamed *Jessica* in 1975 by her new owners, the Pallas Maritime Co., Cyprus. Three years later the vessel was broken-up at Gadani Beach, near Karachi.

The wreck of the motor tanker *Atlantic Duchess* in the Queen's Dock, Swansea, 1951.

The second of February 1951 was a black day in the history of Swansea Docks. In the Queen's Dock lay the Liberian motor tanker *Atlantic Duchess*, her back broken and amidships bridge structure entirely destroyed, and on a 35 degree list.

The tanker, one of a fleet conveying crude oil from Iran to the Llandarcy Refinery, Swansea, was berthed at the Queen's Dock after having discharged her cargo and all pipelines disconnected.

Seven members of her crew were killed, however, following a night-time explosion aboard the ship. Flames from the stricken tanker rose 35 feet into the sky, and the first two explosions rocked the dock area; windows of houses in the vicinity were shattered, and those as far as four miles away were rattled by the force of the explosion. The master of the *Atlantic Duchess* had a lucky escape after being blown across his cabin by the force of the blast.

It was the ship's first trip back to this country. She made her maiden voyage from the builders, William Grey and Co. Ltd., of West Hartlepool, to the Persian Gulf in 1950.

During March, 1951, the bow section of the tanker was towed out of Swansea on the first part of her journey to West Hartlepool where the vessel was to be reconstructed. The stern section followed in April. In 1962 the vessel was renamed *Molat*.

The bow section of the *Atlantic Duchess* leaving Swansea on 21 March 1951, bound for West Hartlepool.

The vessel nearest the camera, (left of the picture) is the 716 gross ton steam tug *Englishman* owned by the United Towing Co. Ltd. She was built by Cochrane & Sons Ltd, Selby in April 1945. She is waiting to take over the tow from the Swansea-based Britannia Steam Towing Co.'s steam tug *Kingforth* (ex. *May Cock,* 1948 and *Flying Falcon,* 1932), built by Ferguson Bros., Port Glasgow in 1904. The masts and part of the funnel of the 359 gross ton steam tug *Superman* can be seen in the centre of the picture, with the 157 gross ton steam tug *Majestic,* built in 1898 by Clelands Graving Dock & Slipway Co. Ltd, Newcastle-on-Tyne, and owned by the Britannia Steam Towing Co. Ltd, Swansea, on the right.

The cargo vessel *Martaban* in the King's Dock, Swansea, 1958.

During September 1952 the 5,740 gross ton cargo vessel *Martaban* was towed into the King's Dock, Swansea, after fire broke out in one of her holds containing 1000 tons of rice, bran, cotton seed, baled cotton and ground-nut oil cake. While berthed against the quay wall the vessel developed a serious starboard list after thousands of gallons of water had been pumped into her.

The *Martaban*, built in 1950 by Wm. Denny at Dumbarton for the British and Burmese Steam Navigation Co. Ltd (P. Henderson and Co.), took on her cargo at Rangoon, unloaded part of it at Avonmouth, and then sailed for Liverpool. Then on discovering the fire in the early hours of the morning, the *Martaban* headed for Mumbles. The Mumbles lifeboat was launched and stood by alongside the burning ship in case of risk to life but, fortunately, no injuries were reported.

At Swansea Docks firemen from Swansea man-handled pumps aboard the pilot cutter *Seamark* and made for the ship, along with the tugs *Clyneforth*, *Waterloo* and *Brockenhurst*. Further assistance came from the B.P. *Firemaster*, the fire float from the Queen's Dock.

The fire was in No. 4 hold and had a firm hold of the cargo. In particular, there was a serious risk from the burning cotton seed because of its oil content, and from the grain because of its tendency to swell under heat. The heat aboard the ship was intense, and both the deck plates and the side of the ship, nearest the hold affected, were so hot that the paint work peeled.

In 1964 the *Martaban* was sold to the China Merchants Steam Navigation Co., Keeling and under the Taiwan flag was renamed *Hai Ho*. Seven years later she was sold by China Merchants Co. Ltd, Taiwan, to Taiwan-based ship-breakers.

HMS *Trondra* (Dispersal Vessel 20) pictured making her way up the river Tawe, probably in 1947, when she was operating from the South Dock, Swansea. Her task was to clear the wreck of the 5,355 gross ton *Fort Médine* (ex. *Bradford City*), which was mined off Mumbles Head in 1941, and for years had been blocking the fairway into Swansea Dock.

HMS *Trondra* was built by John Lewis and Sons of Aberdeen, and launched in October 1941. She was one of the Isle Class trawlers named after islands, and was used to clear shipwrecks which were a danger to shipping in coastal waters and estuaries. The *Trondra* worked in close association with Trinity House and the survey vessel HMS *Seagull*, who together were responsible for the wrecks from Portishead to Milford Haven.

The *Trondra* carried an early type of Asdic set, enabling the pinpointing of wrecks which could later be confirmed by her two motor cutters equipped with echo sounders.

The *Trondra* left Swansea in late 1949 for Plymouth, and was later converted to a boiler-cleaning vessel. She was scrapped at Charlestown in November 1957.

The *Haparangi*, under federal colours, berthed at the King's Dock, Swansea, 1968.

A considerable boost for the Swansea-New Zealand trade was announced in January 1968. An order for 22,000 tons of tinplate for five New Zealand companies was scheduled to be shipped through Swansea Docks. The order would take twelve months to complete with vessels leaving the port for New Zealand about every six weeks.

The tinplate, supplied by the Steel Company of Wales and Richard Thomas & Baldwins, was destined to be used in New Zealand for food packaging and the manufacture of domestic tin ware. Two-thousand tons would be carried at each sailing, and the cargoes would be unloaded at Auckland, Dunedin, Wellington, Christchurch and Napier. The first two vessels, the 14,000 gross ton *Haparangi* and the 11,000 gross ton *Suffolk* loaded the first consignment in January 1968.

The *Haparangi* was built by John Brown & Co., Clydebank, in 1947. She was the first ship of a class of eight built for the New Zealand Shipping Company. She had a capacity of over 500,000 cubic feet of refrigerated space, and 250,000 cubic feet of general cargo space. During 1967 she passed into Federal ownership.

In September 1973 she was sold to Taiwan-based ship-breakers, arriving in Kaohsiung on 6 September 1973.

The *Pieter-S*, the only cargo ship to fly *Y Ddraig Goch* (the Red Dragon).

The m.v. *Pieter-S* was not a large vessel, but she was known to dock workers at the Port of Swansea as the 'polite ship'. This was because the 1,929 gross ton Dutch vessel, captained by John Teumissen of Rotterdam, was the only cargo ship to fly *Y Ddraig Goch*—the Red Dragon—the national flag of Wales. Captain Teumissen explained: 'We always hoist *Y Ddraig Goch* when we enter a Welsh port.' According to the jovial captain, who had spent more than twenty-five years at sea, he bought the flag in Holland.

The *Pieter-S* built in 1954, visited Swansea on 338 occasions, 266 times under the command of Captain Teumissen. It was one of three vessels owned by a Dutch wholesale and retail coal merchant, and the ship took her name from the founder of the company, Pieter Schoonhelm.

In June 1967, the *Pieter-S* was sold to Greek owners and renamed *Nissos Skopelos*. Before being finally beached in Takoradi in July 1978, the vessel bore the following names: *Santa Marina, Santa Eirini, Vasiliki* and *Kritt*.

The *Ulysses* berthed at the King's Dock, Swansea, 1933.

To mark the occasion of the first visit to the port of the s.s. *Ulysses*, one of the Blue Funnel Line, a large number of invited guests took lunch on board the vessel at the King's Dock, Swansea, in 1933. The party, which included many local industrialists, was at the invitation of Messrs. Alfred Holt and Company of Liverpool. Major, the Hon. L. H. Cripps and Major R. H. Thorton, two of the company's managers, flew from Liverpool to Pennard, and then travelled by car to Swansea in order to welcome the guests on board. Not surprisingly, it was commented that their journey emphasised the need for aerodrome facilities to serve Swansea!

The 14,600 gross ton *Ulysses* was built in 1913 by Workman Clark & Co., Belfast. and her twin screws gave her a speed of 14 knots. Her towering funnel rose 75 feet from the boat deck—a feature matched only by the two Cunarder liners, *Saxonia* and *Ivernia*.

The *Ulysses* was normally engaged in general cargo trade, particularly the export of tin-plates and galvanised sheets to the Middle and Far East, although during the early 1930s she had accommodation for 250 first-class passengers who were able to take advantage of the four-month long cruises, visiting four continents. On the occasion of its visit to Swansea the *Ulysses* was on its third major cruise and was fully booked-up for the round trip to the East Indies, Australia, South Africa and home.

Sadly, the *Ulysses* was torpedoed and sunk five miles off Palm Beach, Florida, by the U160 on 11 April 1942. Fortunately, no lives were lost.

The Trinity House tender *Triton* aground near to the South Dock Jetty, 1950 (above) and in Swansea Bay (below).

Listing twenty degrees to starboard, the Trinity House tender *Triton*, is seen grounded in the Tawe near to Swansea's South Dock Jetty in October 1950, her stern firmly embedded in the river bank. *Triton* had been undergoing a major refit at the Cambrian Dry Dock for two months and was being towed by the steam tug *Queenforth* to the King's Dock for a funnel to be fitted when she swung across the river and grounded. After several unsuccessful attempts the vessel was eventually refloated with the aid of three tugs.

Those who saw the film *The Yangtse Incident* may find the lines of this vessel familiar, for the 680 gross ton, coal-fired *Triton* was selected by the film-makers to masquerade as the smokey, Chinese steamer *Kianglang Liberator* in whose wake HMS *Amethyst* took cover during her escape down the Yangtse River. Built as a deep sea trawler by Cochrane & Sons Ltd, Selby in 1940, the *Triton* was taken over during construction and commissioned by the Trinity House fleet as a light-vessel relief and towing vessel. The vessel was broken up in 1963.

HMS *Seraph* and HMS *Sea Scout* in the Prince of Wales Dock, Swansea, 1965.

In December 1965 two 'S' Class submarines of the Second World War—HMS *Seraph* (S.89) (left) and HMS Sea Scout (S. 153) lay silent in the Prince of Wales Dock, Swansea.

The *Seraph* broke adrift on 15 December 1965 while being towed from Portsmouth to Giants Grave, Briton Ferry, by the Admiralty tug *Cyclone*. She was later reconnected to the tug and brought to Swansea Docks. HMS *Seraph*—the cloak and dagger submarine, famous for her launching in 1943 of the body—later known as the 'Man Who Never Was'—off the coast of Spain, seems to have lost her identity as she waits to make her final voyage to the breakers.

She was laid down on 16 August 1940, and launched on 25 October 1941. She figured in many dramatic operations and helped save the lives of thousands of people. During her service she sank a number of small gunboats, enemy coasters and a seaplane. After the war she was used off the south coast of England as a target ship.

HMS *Sea Scout*, also on her way to the breakers at Briton Ferry, was towed into Swansea Bay by the Admiralty tug *Samsonia* on 16 December 1965, and was brought into Swansea Docks, listing badly after receiving a battering in heavy seas. She was built by Cammell Laird and launched on 24 March 1944.

A giant load, destined for the BP oil-refinery at Llandarcy, being unloaded at the Prince of Wales Dock, Swansea, 1952.

Out of the water after a 500 mile sea tow from the Thames, the 105ft. long and 65 ton giant fractioning tower for the catalytic cracker at the Llandarcy oil-refinery extension is being lowered on to timbers on the quayside by the 100-ton and 50-ton floating cranes at the Prince of Wales Dock, Swansea, in February 1952.

The tower was later placed on a railway wagon and then transferred on to a lorry for the road journey to Llandarcy. It took nearly nine hours to complete the three-mile journey from the Queen's Dock, Swansea, to the refinery. The vehicle used to convey the tower weighed 83 tons and it, in turn, was drawn by two tractors, one weighing 18 tons and the other 12 tons.

It took another three days after arrival before the tower was in position. A 100-ton crane fitted with an extra large jib was used to complete the operation.

The *Empire Wapping* berthed at F Shed, King's Dock, Swansea, 1947.

The 2,025 gross ton collier *Empire Wapping* was built in 1945 at Grangemouth Dockyard Co. Ltd, for the Ministry of War Transport. She is pictured at the King's Dock, Swansea, on 1 April 1947, discharging a 1,845 ton cargo of pitwood from Bordeaux destined for distribution to south Wales collieries. While at Swansea she was re-christened *Maystone*, owned by the Thomas Stone (Shipping) Co. Ltd, of Swansea, and named after the wife of the company chairman, Mr. Thomas Stone.

The *Maystone* probably made several voyages to Swansea before her fatal accident on 18 October 1949 when she collided with the aircraft carrier *Albion* during a gale. The accident happened about four miles east of Langstone Light, off the Northumberland coast, when the vessel was bound for Deptford with a cargo of 2,600 tons of coal from Methill, Fife. The *Maystone* sank within five minutes of the collision. Twenty-one of her crew of twenty-five were lost.

The Trinity House vessel *Argus*, pictured at the Prince of Wales Dock, Swansea, in February 1973, was a familiar sight around the Welsh coast for a period of twenty-five years. Mainly employed as a supply vessel, the 2,000 gross ton, twin-screw *Argus*, built by Ferguson Bros. Ltd of Port Glasgow, entered service at the end of the last war and assisted in the clearing of mines off Milford Haven.

She had a long and distinguished career, being called out to assist in a number of rescue operations, including that of the crew of a Dutch coaster which sank off the Welsh coast in a force 8 gale, and also the recovery of a helicopter which crashed into the sea off Holyhead. The *Argus* also earned the reputation, from at least one former crew member, as being one of the best Trinity House vessels. Based mainly at Holyhead, *Argus* was superseded by the *Winston Churchill*.

The final chapter in the history of the *Argus* was written in May 1974, when she sailed into the ship-breakers yard of Thos W. Ward Ltd, at Giants Grave, Briton Ferry.

After being renamed at Birkenhead, the *Hungsia* is seen arriving at the Port of Swansea in April 1973, with the assistance of the Alexandra Towing Company's steam tug *Canning*.

The *Hungsia* is probably better known as the *Demodocus*, an 8,906 gross ton vessel which entered service during August 1955, having been completed by Vickers-Armstrongs Ltd at the Walker Naval Yard on the Tyne. She was the first of a new batch of 'A' Class ships designated Mark V, which had supercharged six-cylinder engines giving her a speed of 16½ knots. She also had accommodation for 12 passengers. The *Demodocus* was transferred to the Glen Line in July 1970 and became the *Glenroy*. The vessel traded under Glen Line colours until 1973 when she returned to the Blue Funnel under her original name.

The ship was renamed *Hungsia* when sold in 1973 to the Nan Yang Shipping Company of Macas, sailing under the Somali Flag. By 1979, however, the ship had become the property of the Peoples Republic of China, and renamed *Hong Q1. 137*.

The 200 gross ton steam tug *Canning* was built in 1954 by Cochrane and Sons Ltd, Selby for the Alexandra Towing Company Ltd. This compact 1,000 h.p. vessel is now a floating exhibit lying alongside Swansea's Maritime and Industrial Museum, at the South Dock.

The oil tanker *Dona Marika* on the rocks at Lindsway Bay, Milford Haven, 1973.

The 11,478 gross ton Liberian tanker *Dona Marika* became a potential time bomb when a storm drove her on to the rocks at Lindsway Bay, Milford Haven, in August 1973.

The vessel had brought 17,000 tons of benzine from Augusta, Sicily, to Milford Haven. After having discharged 12,000 tons of her cargo the vessel was moved to allow another ship to occupy her berth. It was whilst at anchor in Dale Roads, at the harbour entrance, that the *Dona Marika* was pushed aground by gale-force winds and high seas. Villagers from the picturesque village of St. Ishmael's were evacuated because of the risk of explosion from the tanker's cargo of high-octane spirit.

Diesel oil from her engines and some of her highly inflammable cargo were leaking into the sea from a gaping 30-feet hole in her starboard side. It was also feared she was holed along the keel. The air around the stranded tanker was thick with petrol fumes and the main danger was that a spark during recovery operations could set off a massive explosion.

The ship's crew were stranded aboard the vessel despite heroic efforts by the Angle lifeboat to get them off in mountainous seas. They eventually got off the ship with the aid of rope ladders.

After fourteen weeks stranded on the rocks, the tanker was pulled free and refloated with the aid of two Swansea tugs. Extensive repairs to the ship's hull were then carried out, including the fabrication of a false bottom using more than 100 tons of steel.

On 16 November 1973 she was towed to Falmouth by two Swansea tugs—*Mumbles* and *Eggerton*. She was resold to Spanish shipbreakers and arrived in tow at Alicante on 18 December.

The *Dona Marika* was built at Tonsberg in 1954 as the *Thorsorn*, and was owned by A/S Ornen.

Two troopships in the King's Dock, Swansea, 1944.

The successful docking of two large troopships during the duration of one tide was an outstanding event. It occurred on the morning of 2 November 1944 when the 20,614 gross ton troopship *Brazil* (left)—with a length of 586 feet and a beam of 80 feet—arrived at the King's Dock lock, Swansea at 7.00 a.m. She was followed by the 21,329 gross ton, US troopship, *Edmund B. Alexander* (right)—with a length of 668 feet and a beam of 74 feet—which arrived at the King's Dock lock at 8.00 a.m. Both vessels, amongst the largest to have entered the Port of Swansea, carried a full complement of US army officers and other ranks. Twelve trains were arranged for the conveyance of the troops.

Before the end of the same month the *Brazil* took on board five train loads—including two hospital trains—of USA airforce and army personnel and wounded soldiers returning home.

The *Brazil*, originally named *Virginia*, was built in 1928 by the Newport News Shipbuilding and Dry Dock Company, at Newport News, Virginia, and completed for the Panama Pacific Line. In 1938 she had accommodation for 740 passengers, but later underwent extensive alterations which included the removal of her two funnels (the second of which was a dummy) to be replaced by a wider, single funnel. The vessel was renamed *Brazil* and transferred to the American Republic line, a division of the well known Moore McCormack Lines.

In 1941 she was taken over by the US navy and converted into a troopship. The ship was laid up in 1960 and on 28 January 1964 was sold by the US Department of Commerce to the First Ship and Steel Co., New York for demolition.

44

The *British Grenadier*, lying at anchor some two miles off Deal, with crude oil flowing from her damaged side.

Germany's largest liner, the *Bremen*, came into collision with the oil tanker, *British Grenadier*, owned by the British Tanker Company Ltd, in dense fog off Dungeness on 24 April 1930. Fortunately, the main force of the collision was felt between two watertight compartments, and consequently the *British Grenadier* took on very little water, and was able to remain on an even keel. Her bridge on the port side, however, was completely destroyed.

The *British Grenadier*, a regular Swansea trader, was on her homeward voyage from Abadan to Glasgow, with a cargo of crude oil, when the collision happened. Although severely damaged, the tanker was able to proceed to Deal without assistance. The *Bremen* was able to continue her voyage to Southampton without the help of the Dover tugs which had rushed to the scene.

The 6,857 gross ton *British Grenadier* was completed in July 1922, by Swan Hunter and Wigham Richardson Ltd, Wallsend. On 22 May 1941, while on a voyage from Freetown to Aruba, she was torpedoed and sunk by the German submarine U103.

On her maiden voyage in July 1929 the 51,731 gross ton *Bremen*, pride of the German mercantile fleet, wrested the Blue Riband of the Atlantic from the Cunard Line's *Mauretania*. She was built by A. G. Weser, Bremen, Germany, for North Germany Lloyd. She had a service speed of 27 knots, and accommodation for 800 first-class, 500 second-class, 300 tourist and 600 third-class passengers.

In March 1941 she was set afire and scuttled. Her hulk was later broken-up.

The *British Grenadier*'s damaged hull and superstructure.

The captured German U-boat U1023 arriving at Cardiff, 1945.

The captured U1023 submarine—the first to signal its position to the Admiralty after V E Day—arrived at Swansea in June 1945. Her captain was Lt. Commander H. L. Marsham who had left Swansea as a young boy. The submarine toured a number of ports as part of an effort to raise money for King George's Fund for Sailors, and in Swansea members of the public were given the opportunity of seeing all her secrets. During her three-day stay in the North Dock Basin the U1023 was visited by more than 13,000 people, before sailing on to Liverpool.

Her number, painted aggressively on her conning tower, was accompanied by a wolf's head, a logo said to be the insignia of her commander,

known as the Black Wolf. The 500 gross ton, 220 ft long U1023 was one of the German navy's newest submarines and was equipped to remain submerged for up to six weeks.

One of the features of her upper works was the long conning tower, and two gun platforms at the rear. Her guns must have been vicious ones, being a 88mm quick firer, and two other double-barrelled quick-firing flack guns. She was also armed with five torpedo tubes, and capable of cruising 10,000 miles on the surface at a speed of ten knots.

The vessel was commissioned in 1944 and undertook one operational voyage. She sank one vessel.

A demonstration of radio-controlled boats and aircraft staged at the South Dock, Swansea, 1980.
The following buildings can also be clearly identified (from left to right): Swansea Leisure Centre; Weavers & Co.
Ltd; offices of the *South Wales Evening Post*, and the Swansea Industrial and Maritime Museum.

Hundreds of people lined Swansea's South Dock in July 1979 for a demonstration of radio-controlled model boats and aircraft. Organised by the Friends of Swansea Maritime and Industrial Museum, in conjunction with Swansea City Council, the day-long regatta was the first of its kind to be held at the dock.

It was also an experiment to see if it was possible to stage a two-day, radio-controlled, challenge trophy event at the South Dock during 1980. Three local boating clubs took part: Neath & District Model Boat Club, Port Talbot Boat & Yacht Club, and Swansea Model Boat Club. Club members operated radio-controlled, life-size yachts and boats from the quay side. The regatta gave members of the public a chance to see the boats in action before they went on display at the Swansea Model Hobbies and Engineering exhibition held at the Guildhall in July.

Among the treats for onlookers was a superb demonstration of radio-controlled flying by Mr. Alan Beor, of Swansea, with his home-built model of a 'Tyro Major' aircraft. It was the first time he had flown the 4ft 6in wing-span model in Swansea, and during the display it reached up to 40mph.

A sight to remember—the *Prince Ivanhoe*, gaily decked with flags of all colours, quietly making her way back into Swansea after a special celebratory Royal Wedding Day cruise to Ilfracombe and Lundy Island. Five days later, on Monday, 3 August 1981, the *Prince Ivanhoe* was back in the headlines after being involved in a dramatic incident off the Gower coast. During a leisurely cruise along the southern coast of the peninsula the vessel was holed just off Port Eynon Point and had to be hurriedly beached at Horton, where the passengers and crew disembarked.

The sea wasted no time before attacking the deserted vessel, and three months after the accident it seemed hardly credible that the Royal Wedding Day trip had taken place in such style.

The bottle of champagne broke across her stem on 22 February 1951, when she glided down the slip into the River Leven from the Dumbarton yard of Denny Bros. She entered service with British Rail Southern Region on the Portsmouth to Ryde, Isle of Wight, run as a passenger-ferry named *Shanklin*, which was later to carry the Sealink emblem. In 1981 the *Shanklin* became the *Prince Ivanhoe* when she was sold to the Firth of Clyde Steam Packet Co. Ltd, for service on the Clyde alongside the paddle steamer *Waverley*. Prior to her final demise the *Prince Ivanhoe* operated off the South Wales coast, carrying passengers along the Gower coastline. The ship, 200ft in length and latterly displacing 986 gross tons, was diesel powered and had a service speed of 14½ knots.

Pounded by heavy seas the stricken *Prince Ivanhoe* off Horton beach, Gower, October 1981.

Loading scrap on board the cargo vessel *Nicolaos Michalos III* at the King's Dock, Swansea, 1967.

'Operation Scrap' was big business at Swansea Docks during March 1967. Piled high near the main entrance to the port were many thousands of tons of industrial scrap soon to be shipped to China for use in the steel-making process. The cargo, some 10,000 tons, was to be loaded aboard the Greek vessel *Nicolaos Michalos III*. It was one of the largest bulk-loading operations undertaken at Swansea for many years.

The delivery of the scrap to the ship's side was undertaken by Steel Supply (Western) Ltd, of Swansea, operating a shuttle service from the dock entrance, where the scrap was stored, to M Shed at the King's Dock. Engaged in the operation were two lorries—mounted Powell Duffryn Dinosaur units and containers of 20 cu. yards capacity. These containers were discharged at the ship's side where 10 ton grabbing cranes were used to transfer the scrap metal into the holds.

The *Nicolaos Michalos III* was built in 1942 by California Shipbuilding Corporation for the U.S. War Shipping as the *Hubert Howe Bancroft*. The ship was sold by her Greek owners, Mrs. L. C. Michalos and Mrs. S. Ziffos, to Chinese Communist ship-breakers and left Djibouri on 12 May 1967 bound for Whampoa.

The opening of the new extensive Prince of Wales dry dock at Swansea in May 1899 marked a most important development in the commercial history of the town. The dock, the largest of its kind in Swansea, could accommodate two ships at a time and had all the latest facilities, including powerful centrifugal pumps which could empty the basin in about two hours.

Long before midday, the hour at which the opening ceremony was to take place, large crowds had gathered near the entrance gates decorated with streamers. Hundreds more stood on the dock walls. A few minutes before the event, the paddle steamer *Brighton* approached the dry-dock gates, with a few privileged passengers aboard.

The principal guests had assembled at the east mouth of the entrance. Mrs Mawson, wife of the chairman of the company, was conducted on to a bridge stage by Mr. M. Mordey, and presented with a pair of silver scissors. Mrs. Mordey handed her a bouquet of flowers. Mrs. Mawson then proceeded to cut the ribbon to allow the first ship to enter, and in a clear voice said: 'I declare the dock open, and I wish success to the Company'. To more cheering the *Brighton* made her way triumphantly into the dock. Guests aboard the *Brighton* were later entertained by the proprietors, and the dock company provided refreshments in the company's offices.

An impressive vehicle being unloaded off the *Coventry City* berthed at the King's Dock, Swansea, 1967.

Dockers at Swansea had one of their biggest tasks to contend with in March 1967, when a giant 45-ton Mac dumper-trunk was unloaded at the King's Dock from the m.v. *Coventry City* by a 50-ton floating crane, assisted by the motor tug *Cambrian*.

The dumper-truck was brought from New York for a six-month trial period by the National Coal Board, and was moved to the Maes Gwyn open-cast coal site at Glynneath under police escort. The £50,000 truck with its 6 ft high wheels could carry a payload of 70 tons.

The 5,192 gross ton *Coventry City* was built by Wm. Doxford & Sons (S.B.) Ltd, and completed in July 1966 for the Bibby Line of Liverpool. The vessel, like the *Toronto City*, was specially constructed for the North Atlantic and Canadian seaway trade. Her equipment included self-tensioning winches, variable-pitch propeller, automatic steering and bridge-engine control.

In 1974 she was sold to Liberian flag operators and renamed *Ilkon Dalio*. She was renamed *Javron* in 1981 and later sold to Taiwan-based ship-breakers, arriving at Kaohsiung under the name *Bounty III* in 1986.

The new Duke of Edinburgh Dry Dock, Swansea, 1959.

In 1959 the new Duke of Edinburgh Dry Dock, of the Prince of Wales Dry Dock Company, Swansea Limited, was nearing completion. The photograph, taken looking towards the entrance, shows the unique floating caisson gate, the upper deck of which forms a roadway, and the commencement of the cast-iron keel blocks being set on the centre line of the dock. One of the specially designed travelling bilge blocks, capable of being adjusted to suit all vessels can be seen on the floor of the dock (left). The dry dock measures 670 feet by 100 feet and the 92 foot wide entrance is capable of accommodating the largest ship—up to 32,000 tons dead weight— entering the port. The completion of the dock represented the final stage of the development of Palmer's Dockyard, as it was planned when the old dock was built in 1923.

The plaque commemorating the opening of the new dry dock, was unveiled on 3 June 1959, almost sixty years after the company's first dock at Swansea was opened. With the approval of the Queen, the dock was named Duke of Edinburgh Dry Dock by Mrs. Henry Barraclough, wife of Mr. Henry Barraclough, the chairman of the company. The formal opening ceremony was performed by the Hon. T. G. D. Galbraith M.P.. Civil Lord of the Admiralty.

On the right of the picture, in the old Palmer's Dry Dock, is the Blue Funnel motor ship *Antenor* of 7,965 gross tons, completed in July 1956 by Vickers-Armstrong (Shipbuilders) Ltd, Walker-on-Tyne, for the Ocean Steamship Company.

The Porteynon Lifeboatmen's memorial in the village churchyard.

The final drama in the story of the Porteynon Lifeboat was played out on Saturday, 1 January 1916, when the lifeboat *Janet* was launched to help the 236 gross ton Glasgow steamer *Dunvegan* which was riding dangerously near the rocks at Oxwich on the Gower coast.

At 10.30a.m. in the morning news reached Porteynon that a steamship was in difficulties and according to reports there were lives in peril. Undeterred by the strong gale and extremely rough seas, and true to the traditions of their glorious past, the men of Porteynon responded. Most of the village turned out to see the lifeboat set off towards the ship which lay between Oxwich and Pwll-du. For two hours they battled with the high seas in an effort to reach the vessel. They fought hard and long but, realising the impossibility of their task, decided to make for Mumbles.

En route to Mumbles, however, the first disaster befell the lifeboat. The high sea lifted the boat out of the sea, turned her clean over and ripped off the mast. For some time thirteen men were struggling for their lives in the water, but one man, William Harris, who had managed to keep a tight grip on a seat, remained on board. After the boat had righted itself he managed to help some of the crew back on board. The second coxswain William Eynon and his brother-in-law George Harry, however, were missing. Down to eleven men, it was decided to abandon all hope of picking up their comrades and continue the run to Mumbles.

Less than half an hour after the first catastrophe, another huge wave struck the boat broad-side on. Once again the crew were struggling in the water under the upturned boat and when she righted herself, it was discovered that a third member of the crew, William Gibbs, had been washed away. Now without the coxswain and with only seven oars left—the rest had been washed away—the run to Mumbles Head was resumed.

In the gathering gloom they saw the Mumbles Lifeboat pass by a few hundred yards away. A signal, had they had one, would have saved them a night of suffering and anguish, but there was not so much as a match aboard. Then the pilot cutter *Beaufort* sailed passed the weary lifeboatmen. Another steamer passed by, this time within hailing distance, but all efforts to attract her failed.

Finally, at about 7.00a.m. on Sunday, 2 January, after twenty hours at sea and suffering greatly from exposure, the weary crew rounded the pier. Later on Sunday the survivors were taken back to Porteynon by bus.

The disaster prompted the closure of the Porteynon Lifeboat Station.

The *Samtampa* lies split in three on the Sker rocks, near Porthcawl, 1947.

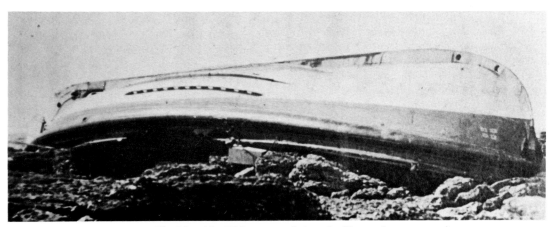

The Mumbles lifeboat upended on the Sker rocks.

On 23 April 1947 all eight members of the Mumbles lifeboat were drowned off Porthcawl when they went to the aid of the doomed crew of the Liberty ship *Samtampa*.

The tragedy began to unfold when the 7,219 gross ton *Samtampa*—built in 1943 by the New England Shipbuilding Corporation of Portland, Maine, as the *Peleg Wadsworth*, and owned by the Ministry of War Transport—was steaming in ballast from Middlesbrough to Newport, where she was to go into dry dock for inspection. Severe weather left her rolling helplessly with engine failure in the Bristol Channel, off Nash Point.

During that fateful afternoon the weather deteriorated and by 5.15p.m. the vessel was aground on the rocky ledge off Sker Point and beginning to break up. She was dwarfed at times by the waves that pounded her side and the rocks around her.

The on-shore rocket apparatus was called for and set up with great difficulty. It was thought the rockets might have provided a means for a safety line to reach the ill-fated vessel but the crew were contemptuously thrown back by the hurricane-force winds. Rescue attempts were made again and again, but to no avail. Battered by the wind and waves, the *Samtampa* was driven further ashore and split in three. As the crew huddled on the bridge, tons of crude oil gushed into the sea, adding a further hazard to rescue attempts.

The Mumbles lifeboat was launched in raging seas as dusk fell, returning after failing to make contact with the ship on her first trip. Once again the *Edward Prince of Wales* braved the storm and battled across Swansea Bay towards Sker Point. Then—silence. Nothing more was seen or heard of the lifeboat until the wreck was found washed ashore on the same rocks which had claimed the *Samtampa*.

The thirty-nine crew members of the *Samtampa* were dead. So too were the lifeboatmen.

On 1 May 1947 the wreck of the lifeboat was burnt after officials of the Royal National Lifeboat Institution realised that the craft was beyond repair. The task of destroying her with the aid of oil, magnesium flares and oil-soaked timber from the *Samtampa*, was undertaken by the Porthcawl Fire Service.

Mumbles, Swansea and the whole of Britain mourned the eight heroic men who gave their lives in the service of others. The memory of that stormy night of 23 April will never been forgotten by the men and women of Mumbles, or the families of the men who stand-by on a constant 24-hour alert to save life at sea.

The *Swansea*, registered at Swansea, seen ashore at Vazon Bay on the west coast of Guernsey during the early 1900s. Among the people congregating round the ship, is a group of women gaily attired in turn-of-the-century costumes, whilst horse-drawn wagons can also be seen hauling coal up the beach from a pile located near the stern section of the ship.

The *Swansea*, a steel-screw steamer of 966 gross tons, was built in 1894 by W. Harkness & Sons of Middlesbrough, and was owned by the Pansey Steam Ship Co. (S. Le Boulanger, Managers), formerly of 13 Cambrian Place, Swansea. In 1907 the *Swansea* was renamed *Lydia*, and under the ownership of Rederi A/B Galedonia was registered at Hlsnborg, Sweden. Although still under the Swedish flag, she was renamed *Valem* in 1939. In 1953, however, after surviving two world wars, she was sold to Danish shipbreakers, and the vessel arrived at Copenhagen, her final destination, on 28 July 1953.

Pictured in her 'home' port loading tinplate for South Africa in August 1958, is the 9,900 gross ton *City of Swansea*, a standard, fast cargo liner built in Glasgow in 1946 for the Ellerman Line. She also set sail on her maiden voyage from Swansea in the same year. Traditionally, Ellerman vessels were named after cities, though Swansea at that time was a town. In the ship's lounge was fixed a bronze plaque bearing Swansea's coat-of-arms, presented by the line's Swansea agents, Burgess and Co. Ltd. Prior to leaving on her maiden voyage, she loaded rails and tinplate in Swansea for the developing South African gold mines.

In 1968, the *City of Swansea* was bought by the Ben Line and renamed *Benkitlan*. She was sold to a Taiwan shipbreaker in 1972, but her plaque and bell were returned to Swansea. At a ceremony held at the Guildhall, the Mayor of Swansea, Councillor Chris Thomas, was presented with both items, together with a photograph of the ship, by Mr. E. R. Newman, the Public Relations Officer of Ellerman Line.

The *City of Swansea* had originally been built as a Ministry of War Transport ship, and according to policy her name had not been inscribed on the ship's bell. During the course of her extensive travels the *City of Swansea* was a fine ambassador for both Swansea and the Ellerman Line. The plaque, bell and photograph are housed in the city's Maritime and Industrial Museum.

The Mayor of Swansea, Councillor Chris Thomas, with the inscribed plaque from the *City of Swansea*, at the Guildhall, Swansea, February 1973.

The steam tug *Queenforth*, owned by the Britannia Steam Towing Co. Ltd, Swansea, was sunk by enemy action at its moorings, at B Shed, King's Dock, presumably by a high-explosive bomb, which fell into the water alongside the vessel in February 1941. An examination of the hull by the company's diver later revealed that the *Queenforth* had not been holed. However, the berth at the King's Dock could not be used until the vessel had been raised.

Fortunately many of the other bombs which fell that night failed to detonate, and although their safe removal posed considerable problems they were far less than would have been the case had they exploded.

In June 1942 the operation of lifting the tug was performed by means of two 45ft-high, stout timber lifting towers located either side of the vessel and resting on the dock bottom. Across the top were bridged iron girders and upon these were rigged the lifting tackle by means of which the tug was heaved clear of the water.

Two days later the *Queenforth* was safely placed on the blocks at the Cambrian Dry Dock, Swansea. After several dockings, the tug was put back into commission in 1943.

The 204 gross ton tug was built in 1911 by Goole Shipbuilding Co. Ltd, Goole. She had a length of 100ft with a draught of 10.4ft. The *Queenforth* left Swansea in 1958 for breaking-up at Llanelli.

The tug *Queenforth* at the Cambrian Dry Dock, Swansea, soon after she had been raised. In the background can be seen the corner of Cambrian Place and Burrows Road.

The *Greystone Castle* berthed in the King's Dock, Swansea, 1951.

Crates containing cars and tractors were lined up on the quayside near M Shed, King's Dock, Swansea, in December 1951, ready for loading aboard the 8,008 gross ton s.s. *Greystoke Castle*, which was destined to transport the 1,500 vehicles to Sydney, Australia. At the time it was probably the largest cargo of cars and tractors to be shipped overseas from the United Kingdom. The cars were supplied by the Standard, Routes, Vauxhall and Ford companies. Around 500 cars arrived in Swansea by road, and a similar number were transported by rail. The remaining cars and Ferguson tractors were in crated sections ready for assembly on arrival.

The *Greystoke Castle*, managed by Hollers, London and chartered by the Standard Motor Co., was owned by the Lancashire Shipping Co., Hong Kong. The vessel was built in 1943 for the U.S. Maritime Commission as the aircraft carrier H.M.S *Trouncer*. It was subsequently reconstructed as a merchant ship, and emerged in 1948 as the *Greystoke Castle* before being renamed *Gallic* while on charter to Shaw Savill & Albion. The ship was finally renamed *Benrinnes* in 1959, and sold in 1973 to Formosan shipbreakers.

Within four days of arriving at the Prince of Wales Dock, Swansea in September 1952 with her cargo of 926 tons of pig iron from Holland, the 746 gross ton *Stream Fisher* sank at her moorings. Water poured into the engine-room through portholes that had been left open while loading a cargo of anthracite coal under number five hoist at the Prince of Wales Dock.

Work was at once stopped and urgent calls made to Swansea Fire Brigade and the Britannia Towing Company's tug *Clyneforth*, which was equipped with pumping apparatus for fire fighting. However, all efforts to raise her proved futile as the volume of water proved too great for the pumps. Fortunately, all the crew of the *Stream Fisher* got ashore before she sank and settled on the bottom of the dock. Equally fortunate was the fact that the sunken vessel caused no obstruction to traffic, or to the working of the docks, prior to being raised in November 1952.

The *Stream Fisher* was built in 1943 by S. P. Austin & Son Ltd, Sunderland, as the *Empire Judy*. She was registered at Barrow and owned by Messrs. James Fisher & Co. In 1970 she was sold to J. H. Ramagge, Panama, and renamed *Ramaida*. The vessel was reported sold in 1977 for breaking-up, possibly in Lisbon.

The *Stream Fisher* almost totally submerged at her berth.

Raising the *Stream Fisher*.

A general view of Port Talbot docks taken from the top platform of No. 1 hoist during the late 1950s. Pictured from left to right are the following vessels: on the buoys, the 3,461 gross ton Swedish m.v. *Kengis*, loaded with a cargo of iron-ore, waiting for a berth at Margam Wharf; the 6,858 gross ton British motor ore-carrier *Oregis*, taking on bunkers, also waits to move to Margam Wharf with an iron-ore cargo; and the 3,503 gross ton Spanish steam-ship *Uribitarie* loads scrap for Spain. On the top right-hand side the British m.v. *Macaulay* is loading a coal cargo for West Africa; the 424 gross ton German motor coaster *Wiking* loads coal for Belfast, and in front of her is the 6,859 gross ton British ore-carrier *Ormsary* taking on stores from a dumb barge, while waiting for a berth at Margam Wharf. Leaving the coal hoist, assisted by two steam tugs of the Alexandra Towing Co., is the 3,658 gross ton *Lsustero*, built in 1919, with approximately 2,000 tons of coal on board bound for Sweden. In the foreground is the motor coaster *Sorned* loaded with coal for Belfast.

An historic moment as the £2.5 million ferry *Innisfallen* berths alongside the new dock terminal in Swansea for the first time on 10 April 1969, at the start of a day-long courtesy visit to the port. The Mayor of Swansea, Councillor David Jenkins was the first person to board the vessel and to accord it a civic welcome. He was accompanied by Swansea Dock's manager Mr. W. G. King and the town clerk, Mr. Iorwerth Watkins.

The B&I's terminal at Swansea was specially built by the British Transport Docks Board, and was known as the Ferry Port. It was designed to cater for the rapid disembarkation of passengers, cars and wheeled freight at any state of the tide and during its first year of operation it was expected to deal with 150,000 passengers, 30,000 cars and 60,000 tons of freight.

The 4,580 ton drive on-drive off, West German-built ferry was able to carry 240 cars and 1,200 passengers, and was owned by the British and Irish Steam Packet Co. Ltd. She had a speed of 24 knots.

The *Innisfallen*'s inaugural voyage to Swansea from Cork was made on 2 May 1969. The master of the vessel was Captain T. Davies, a 53-year-old Lancastrian who, since joining the B&I Line at the end of the last war, had served as mate and master on every vessel of the fleet.

In June 1980 the *Innisfallen* was sold to Township Co. S.A., Panama and renamed *Corsica Viva.*

The *Ayrshire* pictured arriving at the King's Dock lock, Swansea, with the assistance of the steam tug *Clyneforth*. The new Scottish Shire liner *Ayrshire* had just completed trials on the Clyde and the first port of call on the ship's maiden voyage to South Africa was Swansea. Her passage from Scotland was unusually swift, for the ship which left Glasgow on Friday, 3 May 1957 sailed passed Mumbles Head on the following morning.

The *Ayrshire* was registered under the ownership of the Scottish Line (Turnbull, Martin and Company Ltd, Managers) and, like her sister ship *Argyllshire*, carried the normal Clan Line markings. They were both regular callers at the port of Swansea.

The 9,424 gross ton *Ayrshire* was completed in May 1957 by the Greenock Dockyard Company

Ltd. She had a service speed of 16 knots and could accommodate 12 passengers. She also had a considerable refrigerated-cargo capacity.

On 23 March 1965, while on passage from the Mersey to Brisbane, she struck a submerged rock and was beached south of Abd-al-Kuri, at the mouth of the Gulf of Aden, in a badly damaged condition. Although refloated on 26 April 1965, the ship suffered further irreparable damage when strong currents swept her aground.

When acquired by the Britannia Steam Towing Company in August 1951 the tug *Clyneforth* was Swansea's most modern tug. The 262 gross ton vessel was built as the *Empire Minnow* in 1943. In March 1966 she was sold to Greek buyers and renamed *Ena* but was reported broken-up in 1969.

A sea drama ends as the tug *Wallasey* assists the *Tillamook* out of Swansea, 1947.

On 21 May 1947 a small group of people witnessed the departure from Swansea of the 10,488 gross ton American tanker *Tillamook* on the first stage of her long tow back to the US, minus a rudder, by the powerful American tug *Farallon*.

The *Tillamook* originally left Swansea for Abadan, in the Persian Gulf, on 30 November 1946, after unloading a cargo of oil. But trouble lay ahead and messages requesting the help of tugs were received at Mumbles, Land's End and Burnham Coastguard Stations. The Mumbles lifeboat set out when signal flames were seen over Port Talbot, and the Porthcawl rocket apparatus crew along with the Coastguard, with breeches-buoy apparatus, also stood by during the night. Despite being lashed by a storm the tanker's master decided it was safer for the crew of 48 to stay aboard the vessel which had run aground near Sker Point on 1 December 1946.

High seas and rough conditions on 2 December prevented attempts by Swansea tugs to reach the tanker, but the crew of one tug—the *Majestic*, owned by the Britannia Towing Company of Swansea—did get close enough to get a line aboard. The heavy seas, however, caused considerable strain on the line, which eventually snapped.

By 4 December conditions had improved and six Swansea tugs were joined by the Dutch ocean-going tug *Zwarte Zee* in an attempt to refloat the tanker. They battled in difficult conditions for more than five hours to free the ship, but their combined effort was unsuccessful.

The *Tillamook* was eventually refloated on Thursday, 6 February 1947, and towed into Swansea Docks from her anchorage in the bay, south of Port Talbot, by the tug *Twyford* and tugs of the Alexandra Towing Company.

Derek Scott (left), the coxswain of the *William Gammon*, discusses the exercise with Leonard Clark, the Chief Fire Officer, aboard the *Seamark*. In the background are the tugs *Wallasey* and *Alexandra*.

Within minutes of a dramatic 'fire at sea' call from the Mumbles Coastguard in July 1968, Swansea fire and rescue services were in action. The Mumbles lifeboat *William Gammon* was launched, tugs alerted, and the Swansea pilot vessel *Seamark* was on its way to a general cargo ship 'on fire' in Swansea Bay.

There was, however, no real-life rescue, for the general cargo ship was in fact the tug *Alexandra*, which had been supplied by the Alexandra Towing Co. Ltd, at Swansea. The pilot vessel *Seamark* was used as the offshore communications centre and was linked by wireless to the control established at the Dockmaster's office at Swansea. This control was, in turn, linked to the fire brigade's main control which had the responsibility of mobilising personnel and equipment. The fire brigade's equipment was lowered aboard the steam tug *Wallasey*, and the exercise was carried out at low water, to simulate the most difficult conditions in which to launch a rescue. The whole operation was designed to test new arrangements for firefighting at sea.

Unloading nickel-copper matte destined for the Clydach works in 1956.

The s.s. *Bristol City* discharging a cargo of nickel-copper matte from Canada for the Mond Nickel works at Clydach in February 1956. The work was, in fact, delayed by ice and snow which hampered the operation of the hydraulic coal hoists and quayside hydraulic cranes.

Built to the order of the Ministry of War Transport, the *Bristol City* was completed in September 1943 by Wm. Gray & Company Ltd, West Hartlepool as the *Empire Nigel*, one of a number of similar standard ships turned out by the yard. After her completion, the 7,052 gross ton vessel was loaned to the Soviet Union and renamed *Archangelsk*, but in 1946 she was back under the British flag as the *Empire Nigel*.

In 1948 she was sold by the Ministry to W. R. Carpenter, Oversea Shipping Ltd, and registered as *Nandi* at Suva. A year later she was bought by the Bristol City Line (Charles Hill & Sons, Managers), Bristol and renamed *Bristol City*. For the next eight years she served as as regular cargo vessel between the Bristol Channel and Canada. In 1957, however, the *Bristol City* was sold to Yugoslavian shipowners and renamed *Zelengora*.

After 28 years of service and seven name changes, she was finally sold for breaking up at Split, where she arrived on 6 July 1972.

A general cargo scene at Swansea Docks in August 1946 where a 60-ton floating crane is seen loading a war department 0-6-0 saddle tank locomotive No. 75293 aboard the s.s. *Bantria*, at A Shed, King's Dock, bound for Italy. The locomotive was built in 1945 by the Vulcan Foundry at Newton-Le-Willows Works. It was built to a 1942 Hunslet Engine Design and was one of 377 made for the Ministry of Supply between 1943 and 1946 for use in ordnance factories and docks. Many were also exported for use on the continent and North Africa. However, several of the locomotives that were exported returned to Great Britain and were used by the National Coal Board and other industrial concerns. Locomotive No. 71516, similar to the one depicted, is now in service on the Gwili Railway, near Carmarthen, where it is on permanent loan from the Welsh Industrial and Maritime Museum, Cardiff.

The 2,400 gross ton s.s. *Bantria* was built by J. L. Thompson and Sons Ltd, Sunderland, in June 1928 for the Cunard Steam Ship Company Ltd. During 1954 she was sold to Costa Line, Genoa, and renamed *Giorgina Celli*. The vessel was broken up in 1968.

A busy scene at the King's Dock, Swansea on the morning of 30 December 1954. A 50 ton floating crane is being manouvered into position by two steam tugs, *Kingforth* and *Herculaneum* (nearest the camera), so that it can be used to load a cargo of railway wagons aboard the 5,123 gross ton, Palm Line vessel *Ashanti Palm*, bound for West Africa.

In the background (left), loading general cargo at D Shed, is the 8,035 gross ton *Clan Mactavish*, built in June 1949 by the Greenock Dockyard Co. Ltd for Clan Line Steamers. She was one of nine new ships that were built and brought into service during the period 1946-1949. The Clan Line vessels specialised in carrying heavy loads and handling every type of cargo, and the *Clan*

Mactavish was equipped with a derrick capable of handling loads up to 125 tons. After a career of twenty-two years she was sold to China-based shipbreakers.

The 184 gross ton steam tug *Kingforth* was built in 1904 as the *Flying Falcon* and acquired by the Britannia Steam Towing Co., Swansea in May 1948. She remained in their service for thirteen years, before being sold for breaking-up at Passage West in January 1961.

The 192 gross ton *Herculaneum* was launched at Leith in January 1909. She spent much of her working life at Swansea but was sold in 1961 and broken up.

A 50 ton capacity Bessemer converter, destined for the new plant at the Abbey Works, Steel Company of Wales, being prepared to be off-loaded from the 991 gross ton m.v. *Milo* on to a specially constructed rail carriage at the Margam Wharf, Port Talbot Docks in July 1958. The floating crane is assisted by the steam tugs *Harrington* and *Cambrian* of the Alexandra Towing Co. Ltd.

The *Milo* was built in 1953 by Charles Hill and Sons Ltd of Bristol for the Bristol Steam Navigation Co. Ltd. She was one of several Bristol-built ships at the 1953 Spithead Review. Her bridge and funnel were combined as a single unit, and she had no derricks. In 1969 the vessel was sold to J. & A. Gardener Ltd of Glasgow who renamed her *Saint Angus*. Seven years later she was sold to Express Line Shipping Co. of the Maldive Islands and renamed *Lady Maria*. Eventually the vessel became a marine loss after going aground in August 1976.

The steam tugs *Harrington* and *Wallasey* were built in 1903 by J. T. Eltringham and Co. Ltd, South Shields. Both vessels served at Swansea for a considerable time before being broken-up at Thos W. Ward Ltd of Briton Ferry in 1959.

The *Epidauro* aground at the foot of Overton cliffs, Gower, 1913.

The s.s. *Epidauro* was on a voyage from the Mediterranean to Swansea, in ballast to load coal, when she ran aground in thick fog on the morning of 13 February 1913 beneath the shadow of Overton Cliffs near Port Eynon. Those slumbering in their beds on shore were roused by the sound of the ship's siren and the firing of rockets, later augmented by the cries of the crew who did not know where they were, or the seriousness of their plight.

Four men put ashore in one of the lifeboats in order to establish their whereabouts, and to organize a rescue party. On reaching the shore they were greeted by the villagers of Port Eynon. The local lifeboat was called out just as a second boat with two men on board, put to sea. Unfortunately, this one met the same fate as the steamer, the men having to scramble to safety. On coming ashore the two sailors were met by Mr Charles Bevan and Mr Francis Taylor, both members of the Port Eynon lifeboat crew. The four then decided to man one of the steamer's lifeboats and pursue the Port Eynon lifeboat which was, by this time, well on its way to the *Epidauro*. On arriving, however, their little craft was swamped by the sea throwing the crew into the ice-cold waters. Fortunately, all four were good swimmers and were picked up by the Port Eynon lifeboat.

By now crowds had gathered on the cliff top and a line was attached to the boat. During the afternoon it was found that the tide had receded sufficiently to enable the crew to walk ashore. But the master, Captain Bete, refused to leave his ship. The lifeline was therefore kept in position, with the breeches-buoy attached, in case anything should happen during the night to force the captain to abandon his ship. The following morning the vessel was deemed to be a total wreck, her back having broken. But, thanks to the gallant efforts of the locals, the lives of all twenty-seven crew members were saved.

The 2,095 gross ton *Epidauro*, formerly the *Hartington*, was built by Palmers & Co. Ltd of Newcastle in December 1883 for the Hudson Steam Ship Co. Ltd.

The *Tours* in Deepslade Bay, Gower, 1918.

The s.s. *Tours*, which had been lying on the rocks at Deepslade Bay, Pennard, Gower for almost eight months, was successfully refloated on Sunday evening, 29 June 1919. It was the climax to a wonderful piece of salvage work.

American-built and owned by La Societe Maritime Auxillaire le Transporte, Paris, the *Tours* was bound for Swansea light to load coal for Nantes when she was driven ashore broadside-on on the rugged Gower coast. The recently built vessel was regarded by her owners as a total wreck. In fact, the 'wreck' was sold to Messrs. C. M. Peel for £1,200.

It was then that a Mr. Towers became involved. He was of the opinion that the *Tours* could be refloated and a salvage syndicate purchased the ship for £4,500.

In March 1919 two unsuccessful attempts were made to get the steamer off the rocks by means of tugs, assisted by a shore engine. But Mr. Towers, who supervised the operation, refused to give up hope and after blasting some of the offending rocks, and with the aid of a high tide, the final and successful effort to free the ship was made. Three tugs, the *Challenger, Staghound* and *Foxhound*, were in attendance in the bay, while on the cliffs and grassy slopes hundreds of people watched the salvage work.

However, the operation, directed on board by Mr. Towers and Captain Jack Davies, almost came to an abrupt halt when an alarming incident interrupted their work. Men were engaged blasting away timbers that kept the ship propped-up on the seaward side when suddenly, without any warning, the steamer slid down the greasy slipway a distance of 40 to 50 feet. Those on shore thought she was going to topple over but, on entering the sea, the cushion of water kept her in an upright position.

An hour to high water and the hawsers were attached to the tugs, and the signal to pull was given. The bow of the *Tours* was lifted by the rising tide. The tug *Challenger* gradually drew the steamer's bow round to point seawards. A flag at the mizzen mast then told the *Staghound* and *Foxhound* to pull on their hawsers and, amid the hearty cheers of the crowd on shore, the *Tours* glided gently into deep water and was towed into Swansea for dry-dock repairs.

72

The Royal Yacht *Britannia* in Swansea Bay, 1969.

In July 1969 thousands of sightseers sought vantage points in order to get a good view of the Royal Yacht *Britannia* in Swansea Bay. The vessel became even more of a spectacle after dark for it was illuminated from stem to stern, a glittering toy-like shape on the calm sea. Her 'guardian', the guided-missile destroyer HMS *Glamorgan*, which had loomed grey and formidable abeam the yacht in the early evening mist, was also spectacularly lit.

In the carnival atmosphere of the evening, yachts and pleasure craft surrounded the Royal Yacht anchored a mile off shore. Even the Mumbles lifeboat joined in for a close-up view of the ship. Traffic reached bank-holiday proportions on the Mumbles Road and car parks at Oystermouth and Bracelet Bay were full. Crowds which had gathered on the cliff behind the Pier Hotel from the moment the Royal Yacht had entered Swansea Bay in the afternoon were still there late into the night. Many visitors also had their first

glimpse of the ferry *Innisfallen*, also lit up as she sailed for Cork.

The Royal Yacht arrived at Swansea ready to receive Prince Charles after his visit to Swansea. The Prince was driven to the new Swansea Ferry Port and transported to the *Britannia* by the Royal barge. He returned to the terminal the following morning to continue his Investiture tour to Neath and Cardiff by road.

As part of the Investiture celebrations four naval ships also visited Swansea Docks: HMS *Defender*, a Daring class destroyer; the submarine HMS *Onyx*; HMS *Andrew*, an A-class submarine completed in 1948, and HMS *Glamorgan*.

The *Britannia* was built by John Brown and Co. Ltd, Clydebank and launched by the Queen on 16 April 1953. With a load displacement of about 4,000 tons, the yacht has a length of 413ft. and a beam of 55ft.

The tug *Gower* making her way down the Queen's Dock, Swansea, 1981.

After a twenty-three hour journey from Liverpool, a new 165 gross ton tug, ordered by the Alexandra Towing Company sailed into Swansea docks in August 1961. Like other vessels owned by the company she bore a local name, *Gower*.

The *Gower* was one of the first ship-handling tugs, built for operation in United Kingdom waters, to be fitted with a controllable pitch propeller. She was built at Northwich, Cheshire by W. J. Yarwood and Sons and the vessel incorporated her owner's ideas and long experience in handling and berthing ships of all sizes in restricted docks at Liverpool, Southampton and Swansea.

At the owner's request, accommodation of a high standard was also provided for a crew of eight.

Separate cabins, situated in the fore end of the deckhouse, were arranged for the master, chief engineer, mate and second engineer. An additional noticeable feature of the vessel is the wheelhouse, raised on the bridge deck and designed to give good all-round visibility. The *Gower* was also fitted with up-to-date equipment: radar, VHF radio, fire and salvage pumps.

In September 1985 the *Gower* was sold to the Greek shipping company Coastas Karolides and left Swansea for the last time on 11 September 1985, bound for Southampton where she was to be dry-docked before completing the last part of her journey to Athens.

HMS *Sheffield* making her way across Swansea Bay in March 1976.

When the *Sheffield* came to Swansea, not long after being commissioned in March 1976, her visit aroused considerable interest as she was the lead ship of a new class of Type-42 destroyers. Ordered in November 1968 and completed in 1975, the 3,500 gross ton *Sheffield* had a length of 420ft and a beam of 47ft. She was also the first destroyer in the Royal Navy to be propelled solely by gas turbines. Her armaments included an automatic rapid-fire 4.5 inch gun, anti-submarine torpedo tubes and the new Sea Dart missile system. Those who admired her lines as she steamed across Swansea Bay would also have noted her 'bedstead' early-warning radar, capable of detecting aircraft at considerable distances.

HMS *Sheffield* was one of two Type-42 guided-missile destroyers lost when hit by an Exocet missile fired by an Argentine aircraft on 4 May 1982, during the Falkland Islands War. The missile hit the *Sheffield*'s control room causing extensive damage. The ship subsequently caught fire and was later abandoned by her crew.

It was ironic that the *Sheffield* should have fallen victim to an air-launched Exocet missile for she was designed to fulfil an air defence role, for which purpose the vessel was fitted with the then new Sea Dart medium-range surface-to-air missile.

HMS *Antelope* arriving at the Port of Swansea in October 1981.

After a forty-eight hour battering by storm-force winds off the Gower coast, the frigate HMS *Antelope*, which was to have put into Swansea on the Thursday, 10 October 1981 for a five-day courtesy visit, finally berthed on the Saturday, 12 October.

Inevitably the round of social engagements arranged for the visit had to be curtailed but a number of sporting events did go ahead. It was, nevertheless, a memorable visit and one which impressed the then Mayor, Councillor Paul Valerio. Over 600 people went aboard the ship during the few hours she was open to the public and many more met crew members through the various events organised ashore.

The 2,815 gross ton *Antelope* was the second of eight ships of the Amazon Class. Her armaments included a singe 4.5 inch gun, anti-submarine torpedo tubes, Seacat anti-aircraft missiles and a Lynx helicopter.

A few months before visiting Swansea HMS *Antelope* was in the headlines following her interception of a coaster off Balize found to be carrying a cargo of illegal drugs worth £30 million.

Like HMS *Sheffield*, HMS *Antelope* was a victim of the Falklands War. The vessel sank after being badly damaged by Argentinian bombs on Sunday, 23 May 1982 when the Argentine Air Force resumed its raid on San Carlos Bay. Although only a few planes broke through the defensive screen *Antelope* suffered direct hits which were to have such devastating consequences.

The *Ramo* berthed at the King's Dock, Swansea, 1976.

A great deal of interest was created at Swansea Docks in 1976 when the Panamanian m.v. *Ramo*, bearing the *Playboy* insignia on its funnel, berthed at King's Dock. Dockers and members of the public alike crowded around to have a peep at the 2,000 gross ton vessel, hoping to catch a glimpse of international playboy Hugh Heffner and his female companions. But if they really did expect to see a beauty-laden bunny boat they were very much disappointed. For the only figures to emerge were brawny crewmen, and the only cargo, steel coils!

The rabbit's head, complete with black bow-tie, had a different meaning to that usually associated with the Heffner *Playboy* empire. The sign, as Captain Jimmy Bootsma explained, was painted 'more or less' as a practical joke. 'Every time they used to return to Panama, the crew used to put their fingers up at either side of their heads to say ''Hello'' to the locals. But when they painted the bunny sign to mean the same thing, Hugh Heffner complained,' said Captain Bootsma.

Despite Heffner's protests, the bunny was allowed to stay and it created interest everywhere they went.

Owned by Rosedene Shipping S. A. Panama, the *Ramo* was abandoned by her crew on 29 November 1980 after a fire had broken out in her engine room when she was about 50 miles south-east of Victoria, during a voyage from Asuncion to Rotterdam. The gutted vessel was taken in tow and brought into Victoria on 2 December 1980.

Captain Jimmy Bootsma and his Black Bunny.

Floating cranes loading a 115 ton cargo on board the *Montreal City* at the King's Dock, Swansea, 1959.

Two record 'lifts', each of about 115 tons, were made by two cranes at the Port of Swansea in June 1959. Both were part of a consignment of machinery which was being loaded aboard the s.s. *Montreal City*. The deck of the 7,145 gross ton vessel had been specially strengthened to carry the great weight of the American-made slabbing mill, which had been installed at the Steel Company of Wales's Abbey Works in 1951 but was now being replaced by more up-to-date equipment.

Sixty rail trucks, apart from road vehicles used for the major items, were required to transport the cargo from the Abbey Works, Port Talbot to the King's Dock, Swansea. To assist in the loading the British Transport Commission called upon the help of the 100 ton floating crane *Simson III*.

The mill, which had taken twelve weeks to pack, had been purchased by a Pittsburgh firm of dealers in industrial plant and rolling mills and was destined to be transported by the *Montreal City* to the extreme western end of the St. Lawrence Seaway, for discharge at Duluth.

The *Montreal City*, formerly the *Fairmount Park* owned by the Canadian Government, was built by the Busrard Dry Dock Company, Vancouver in 1945. In 1946 she was purchased by Bristol City Line and renamed *Montreal City*. In 1959 she was sold to the Polish Government and renamed *Huta Baildon*. The vessel was finally broken-up at Gdansk, Poland in 1974.

HMS *Crossbow* arriving at the Port of Swansea, 1953.

To coincide with the visit of the Queen and Duke of Edinburgh to Swansea in July 1953, two destroyers —HMS *Battleaxe* and HMS *Crossbow*—took up berths in the Prince of Wales Dock. Both vessels were open to the public.

Their arrival in Mumbles Road was the occasion for an exchange of signals of greetings between the Mayor of Swansea, Councillor D. S. Fisher and the commanding officers of the destroyers, Captain E. C. Bayldon of the *Battleaxe* and Commander C. D. Maddon of the *Crossbow*. Both officers called on the mayor at the Guildhall and the mayor and mayoress later went aboard the *Battleaxe* for lunch.

Sailors lined the route of the royal procession through the town and were to be the guests of Swansea at several functions. Theatres and cinemas had been generous in their allocation of free seats to members of the two crews and there were also tours of Gower and tea parties at the Guildhall for the ratings.

HMS *Crossbow* was launched in December 1945 and completed in March 1948. She formed part of the 6th Destroyer Flotilla (later squadron) until 1955, when she was placed in reserve. After being recommissioned in 1959, *Crossbow* spent much of her time in Mediterranean waters but in 1966 she was converted into a harbour training ship for mechanical engineers, based at Portsmouth. The 2,287 gross ton HMS *Crossbow*, which never fired a shot in anger, made her last voyage to Thos. W. Ward's shipbreaking yard at Giant's Grave, Briton Ferry, in January 1972.

The *Clan Davidson* berthed at the King's Dock, Swansea, 1956.

Following the outbreak of the Second World War the Ministry of Shipping, which was later to become the Ministry of War Transport, took control of all merchant shipping and it was not long before Clan Line ships were calling at ports on unfamiliar routes and carrying strange cargoes. Since all routes passed through areas menaced by German submarines or aircraft, it seems invidious to pick out individual deeds, but perhaps one example will serve to show the valuable contribution merchant shipping made to the war effort.

The *Clan Davidson*, the ship on which the book and film *Above Us The Waves* was based, arrived at the King's Dock, Swansea in 1956 and caused a stir among dock workers. Initially, the interest shown in her was no more than that usually given to vessels which had not visited the port before or which had not docked in Swansea for several years. But that was soon to change when dock workers encountered in the ship's smoke room a crest bearing what seemed to be a Welsh dragon on a horseshoe below the name 'Bonaventure'. Alongside was the following inscription: 'This crest was carried on this ship during the Second World War when she

was engaged in successful exploits as a parent ship to secret midget submarines.' On the reverse side of the crest was a list of some of the *Bonaventure*'s exploits which included: '*Tirpitz* crippled, Altensfjord 1943; *Takao* sunk, Singapore 1945; Bergen floating dock destroyed; cut main Japanese telegraph cables between Singapore and Japanese mainland.'

Below the crest was the simply worded record: 'In the above actions the submarine crews won four VCs, sixteen DSOs and 40 other awards for gallantry.'

Originally built as a Clan Liner early in the Second World War, the 8,067 gross ton *Clan Davidson* was taken over by the Admiralty to act as midget-submarine depot ship under the name *Bonaventure*. For the remainder of the war she served in that capacity and it was not until 1948 that she resumed her role as part of the merchant fleet. Whilst at Swansea in 1956 the ship loaded a general cargo bound for Bombay and Calcutta. The *Clan Davidson* made her last voyage from Glasgow and Liverpool to Columbo, arriving there in November 1961.

The *Grace Harwar* berthed at the Prince of Wales Dock, Swansea, 1929.

The *Grace Harwar* was a steel, full-rigged ship of 1,877 gross tons built in 1889 by Hamilton of Port Glasgow for Montgomery of London. In August 1927 the vessel left Swansea on the first leg of a round trip to Australia, a voyage dogged by a series of mishaps. The passage to Luderitz Bay, South West Africa, lasted 65 days but six days before arrival, Captain Svenson fell and broke his leg and was hospital bound for 70 days. When the ship eventually put to sea again bound for Peru, the Captain was still on crutches: 'Not a good rig,' he remarked, 'for the Roaring Forties!' But while in Peru, loading guano for North Carolina, dysentry struck the crew and the sailmaker died.

From Carolina the *Grace Harwar* went in ballast to Australia. On 17 March 1928 the vessel, with a cargo of wheat on board, left Australia on the first leg of a voyage which was to last 138 days, but during the first week half a dozen sails were blown out, and the ship met constant headwinds and hurricane-like squalls. It was impossible to round the South Island of New Zealand, so they sailed through Cook Strait, the dangerous passage between the two islands seldom attempted by large sailing ships. Fortunately, that passage was successfully negotiated but more problems lay ahead.

At 4 o'clock on the morning of 25 May halfway to Cape Horn, an Australian journalist was killed whilst adjusting the sails during a storm. He was buried at sea the next day.

Going round Cape Horn the weather deteriorated but the ship, although 40 years old, fought gamely. Several times quantities of fish oil had to be poured around the ship to calm the sea.

A week or so later, worse was to follow. According to the captain, 'One of the crew became deranged. He came out one afternoon on his free watch. I was on the bridge. He called out to me: "Goodbye, Captain" and jumped overboard.' Although unconscious when rescued the man resumed his duties after a fortnight's rest.

The *Grace Harwar* finally docked in Queenstown, Tasmania on 3 September 1928, where the captain decided to take a well earned rest.

In 1935 the vessel was sold to Scottish shipbreakers for £2,150.

The elegant *Kathleen & May* drying her sails in the Weaver's Basin, Swansea during the late 1950s. In the foreground (left) is the bow section of the sailing ketch *Emily Barratt*.

To the end of her days the 136 gross ton *Kathleen & May* carried a prayer which was inscribed over the saloon: 'God protect the Kathleen & May'. The vessel first took to the waters in April 1909 and left Ferguson and Bairds yard at Connah's Quay, near Chester, as the *Lizzie May*, named after the two daughters of her owners. But on passing into Irish hands in 1908 her name was changed to *Kathleen & May* after two members of her new owner's family.

An £800 refit in 1931 saw the installation of an 80bhp engine and changes to her rigging. More powerful engines were installed in 1947, and again in 1952.

During the 1930s she worked the Bristol Channel and Irish trade and was particularly involved in the shipment of cargos of Welsh coal. And in Captain Tommy Jewell the *Kathleen & May* had an owner-skipper who gave her the attention that became a legend around the coasts.

Besides going aground on the Goodwin Sands in 1908 her only serious accident happened in July 1947 when she was involved in a collision with the trawler *Tenby Castle* at Swansea.

After being sold for £4,000 in 1961 the *Kathleen & May* changed hands several times. From July 1966 to June 1967 she remained at Barry before being transferred to Appledore. She lay in the Torridge for three years until purchased by the newly formed Maritime Trust who saw her in the spring of 1970. The three-masted topsail schooner *Kathleen & May* is now berthed at the St. Mary Avery Dock, Southwark, London.

The *Gloucester City* discharging heavy machinery, probably at Newport Docks, during the late 1930s.

Captain Sydney Smith, born and bred in Swansea, was one of the youngest Master Mariners in the Merchant Navy and his role in saving the victims of German raids during the Second World War won him the OBE. During a period of four months his ship, the 3,071 gross ton *Gloucester City*, had saved the lives of 135 men, the survivors from merchant ships attacked by the enemy in mid-Atlantic.

Captain Smith lived as a boy in Windsor Street, Swansea, and he went to sea at the age of 15. It was not long before he realised his boyhood ambition to command his own ship, and in that capacity he earned the respect of his colleagues. On more than one occasion he personally attended to injured crew members and survivors.

The *Gloucester City* was built in 1919 by J. Blumer & Co., Sunderland, for the Prince Line, having been laid down as the *War Planet*. In 1936 she was renamed *Moorish Prince* and in that same year was acquired by Bristol City Line and renamed *Gloucester City*. In 1949 the vessel was sold to South African Lines and renamed *Namaqualand*. Two years later she was purchased by a Pakistani company and renamed *Kaderbalesh*. After serving her various owners over a period of 42 years she was sold for breaking-up at Karachi in 1961.

The tanker *British Princess*, the chosen location for a documentary film.

In September 1961 Swansea was the location chosen for filming a documentary called 'Fire Down Below', which the British Petroleum Company was making on behalf of the Shipping Federation. The film was not concerned with fires on tankers as such, but with fires in all kinds of ships, and especially those affecting accommodation quarters.

The film was set against the background of an official court of inquiry into the abandonment and loss of a ship as a result of fire, although no real fire was started aboard the 'stricken' vessel. A number of actors were used, but most of the crew were played by professional seamen.

The 8,000 gross ton tanker *British Princess* was deemed a suitable location simply because the company had easy access to her and she was about to be sent to Thos W. Ward Ltd, Briton Ferry, for demolition.

The motor tanker *British Princess* was built by Sir J. Laing and Sons Ltd, Sunderland, for the British Tanker Company and launched by Princess Elizabeth in 1946.

The stricken *Jens-S* entering the King's Dock, Swansea, 1967.

A German timber ship, listing heavily to starboard, was towed into Swansea Docks on Monday, 31 July 1967, after a dramatic fight to save it from sinking in the Bristol Channel. The 499 gross ton *Jens-S* had been taken in tow by the Mumbles lifeboat *William Gammon*, assisted by the coastal tanker *Shell Steelmaker*, after the stricken vessel had been located several miles south-east of the Scarweather lightship. Two tugs later took over the towing as the eight-man crew of *Jens-S* tried frantically to lessen the heavy list by throwing timber into the sea. Plans had been made to beach the ship at Oystermouth but the Swansea-based tugs *Talbot* and *Cambrian*, under the command of Captain Jack Williams and Captain Jack Fethney, reported that the jettisoning

of the cargo, which left a trail of timber in her wake, had improved the ship's position to a list of 20° to starboard, and that the *Jens-S* was being towed into Swansea Docks.

The Mumbles lifeboat, however, kept watch on the scene, and stood by to take off the crew if the situation deteriorated. With the *Jens-S* making 'good progress' nearing Mumbles Head, pilots aboard the *Seamark* also went out to meet the vessel, which had been heading for Sharpness on the River Severn.

On 8 December 1971, under the name *Susan*, she foundered and sank in heavy seas while on a voyage from Granville to Aarhus. There were no survivors from her crew of four.

The end of an era at Swansea South Dock, 1971.

At noon on Monday, 31 May 1971 the swing bridge in Swansea's South Dock closed for the last time. With the movement of three levers, lock-gate man Mr. Les Watson swung the 66 year-old bridge between the dock and its basin for the last time, so ending a long chapter in the history of the Port of Swansea. Mr. Watson, who had been responsible for the bridge for nearly twenty-five years, said: 'This was the saddest job I've been asked to do since working on the dock.' His sentiments were echoed by the crowds of sightseers who had also come to bid their farewell.

The last vessel to sail out through the passageway from the South Dock to the basin was the luxury yacht *Fairwood* (pictured), owned by Mr. S. J. Jeffrey of Gower Road, Upper Killay, Swansea. As Mr. Watson swung the bridge open, Swansea Dock Master, Captain Jack White, and his assistant, Captain T. Chappell, cast off the *Fairwood* for her ceremonial trip around the South Dock before heading gently and silently out through the passageway. With the owner at the wheel, the white and blue yacht made an impressive sight against the darkened sky. On board the *Fairwood* were Swansea's Mayor and Mayoress, Councillor and Mrs. Ken Hare, the town clerk, Mr. Iorwerth Watkins, accompanied by Mrs. Watkins, dock manager, Mr. Bill King and Mrs. King, Mrs White and Mrs. Jeffreys.

However, it was not the first time that the yacht had taken part in ceremonial occasions. In 1969 it served as a base and home for Lord Snowdon while he was at the Investiture at Caernarfon.

Mr. Jeffreys bought the *Fairwood* in 1961. It was built to his own specifications with automatic pilot, radar and stabilisers. The vessel weighed 98 gross tons and had a cruising range of 4,000 miles.

The *City of Paris* berthed at the King's Dock, Swansea, 1933.

In October 1933 more than 200 India-bound passengers on board the Ellerman Line *City of Paris* were stranded in Swansea after their ship limped into port. The 11,973 gross ton liner had left Liverpool on Friday, 6 October, but whilst sailing down St. George's Channel on the Saturday morning the ship developed engine trouble. After completing temporary repairs, the owners instructed Captain Jackson to make for Swansea, the nearest large port, to complete the work.

The local agents, Messrs. Burgess & Co. and Messrs. Palmer's Dry Dock Company at Swansea, as well as the Alexandra Towing Co. Ltd, were contacted immediately and all necessary arrangements were made for docking the liner and seeing to the needs of the passengers.

Meanwhile, Mr. A. G. Workman—one of the directors of the Ellerman Line who had arrived at Swansea from Liverpool—and Mr. McGregor,

manager of Palmer's Dry Dock put to sea in the steam tug *Herculaneum* on the Saturday evening in order to meet the liner in Mumbles Roads. After examining the damage to the vessel, three tugs, *Herculaneum, Wallasey* and *Hornby,* took the liner in tow and she was berthed at 3 Quay, King's Dock.

On board the *City of Paris* were 196 officers and crew, and 211 passengers, some of whom took advantage of the few extra day ashore to visit friends at Bristol and elsewhere. Others spent their time sight-seeing in Swansea. A drive to Oxwich and Penrice Castle was also arranged, as too were cinema visits and a concert party on board.

The vessel finally left Swansea on Wednesday, 11 October 1933.

The *City of Paris* was built in 1921 at Wallsend-on-Tyne by Swan Hunter and Wigham Richardson Ltd. On 28 February 1956 she arrived at Newport, Gwent, for breaking-up by John Cashmore Ltd.

The Cunard Liner *Laconia* anchored off Mumbles, 1930.

Delayed by stormy weather, the Cunard liner *Laconia*, under the command of Captain Protheroe, dropped anchor about half-a-mile from the Mumbles Pier shortly before 5p.m. on Sunday, 3 August 1930. On board were passengers from America who were on their way to the National Eisteddfod at Llanelli. Large crowds gathered at Mumbles and other vantage points to witness the arrival of the vessel as she steamed up-channel flying the Welsh flag on her foremast. Furthermore, the arrival of the tender *Skirmisher* at the King's Dock with the Welsh-Americans on board was also greeted by thousands of people who had lined the entire length of the West Pier and the dockside. As the tender berthed a choir conducted by Mr. W. J. Jones struck up the Welsh National Anthem followed by 'Cwm Rhondda'. The passengers were formally welcomed ashore by the Mayor and Mayoress of Swansea, Councillor and Mrs. T. A.

Lovell, the Mayor and Mayoress of Llanelli, the town clerk of Llanelli and Eisteddfod officials.

There were many touching scenes as relatives and friends were reunited after many years separation. Especially poignant was the experience of eight year old Gladys Irene Williams from Warrensville, Ohio. She made the voyage by herself in order to visit her grandparents, Mr. and Mrs. Jones of Midland Terrace, St. Thomas, Swansea.

The 19,695 gross ton *Laconia*, the largest liner to have disembarked passengers at Swansea, was built by Swan, Hunter and Wigham Richardson Ltd, Newcastle-on-Tyne and completed January 1922. Sadly, the vessel met her end homeward-bound from Egypt in September 1942 when she was torpedoed by the U156 some 700 miles south-west of Freetown, Sierra Leone.

The *Moelfre Rose*.

The 631 gross ton, steam coaster *Moelfre Rose* arrived at the Prince of Wales Dock, Swansea on Sunday, 21 December 1958, after battling against gales for 70 hours. She had travelled from Liverpool and was brought to Swansea under tow by the tug *Margam*, a new addition to the Alexandra Towing Company's fleet. Her arrival intact was a tribute to the seamanship of Liverpool tugboat skipper, Captain H. Wright, who returned by train to Liverpool with his crew on the following Monday. The only person aboard the coaster at the Prince of Wales Dock was Mr. Taliesin Owen, of Anglesey. He had served as the mate on the ship for 13 years. During that time, the *Moelfre Rose* had been engaged in the West Country clay trade, the Irish coal and potato trade, and had carried grain and timber to and from Continental ports.

At the height of the gale, the tug and her 27-year-old charge were driven towards the Irish coast near the Black Water shoal and the Black Water light vessel. Because the *Moelfre Rose* was shipping water the pumps were kept going hour after hour, and

distress rockets were fired in case assistance would be required. In fact, the Arklow lifeboat was launched, an RAF Shackleton aircraft took off from Ballykelly, Northern Ireland, and the Royal Navy frigate *Llandaff* proceeded to the area, but a change in wind direction averted a crisis and the tug was able to take the ship clear of the Irish coast before steaming towards St. David's Pembrokeshire. From there on the tug continued to battle against heavy seas and strong winds, conditions which prevented her crew from getting much sleep or food.

The *Moelfre Rose* remained at Swansea until tidal conditions at the mouth of the river Neath enabled her to make her final port of call—the breakers yard on the seaward side of the Neath River Bridge. She was probably the first ship to be broken up at the yard owned by the Steel Supply Company.

The *Moelfre Rose*, built in 1931, was owned by Richard Hughes & Co. (Liverpool) Ltd but during the early 1950s the company was taken over by Mr. Philip Holden of Swansea.

The aftermath of the disastrous fire at Messrs Weaver and Company's Flour Mills, Swansea, 1926.

One of the most disastrous fires to occur in Swansea broke out at Messrs. Weaver and Company's Flour Mills, North Dock, soon after midnight on Thursday, 24 June 1926. Flames shot high into the air and could be seen for miles around. The fire spread so rapidly that the entire south side of the quadrangular buildings was destroyed, together with offices on the eastern corner. Furthermore the entire stock of stores and most of the company's lorries were also damaged beyond repair.

Across the North Dock, the heat had been so intense that windows were shattered in the smaller mill, near the Lion Stores. A number of railway wagons on the high-level sidings were also destroyed. And worst of all, the single-span overhead bridge (top right) connecting the main mills with the huge grain silo was in danger of falling into Harbour Road. Not surprisingly, the company's engineers, in consultation with the Swansea Corporation Authorities, decided, in the interest of public safety, to close the road which ran under the bridge and divert all traffic and pedestrians.

The *Angel Gabriel* aground!

A fully-loaded Greek tanker which ran aground after leaving the Queen's Dock, Swansea on the evening tide of Wednesday, 1 January 1969, restricted shipping in and out of the port. On the following day seven tugs attempted to release the 12,223 gross ton *Angel Gabriel*, on charter to the BP Tanker Company, but to no avail.

There were fears that the *Angel Gabriel* loaded with about 18,000 tons of fuel oil from the BP Refinery at Llandarcy, might have been damaged, and there were hurried consultations among British Transport Docks Board officials over the dangers of oil spillage. Fortunately, however, that was not so for the tanker, bound for Tranmere and Eastham, had run aground on the muddy west bank after a fault had developed in its stearing gear.

After two earlier attempts to refloat the tanker had failed she was successfully refloated on the evening tide of Thursday, 2 January, after more than 1,000 tons of fuel oil had been pumped from the vessel in order to lighten her load. Following her departure ships anchored in the bay were once more able to enter the port unhindered.

The motor tanker *Angel Gabriel*, formerly the *Alva Star*, was built by Sir J. Laing & Sons Ltd, Sunderland in June 1953 and was owned by the Alva Steam Ship Company Ltd. While on a voyage from Venice to Malta she was driven aground by hurricane-force winds at Marsakala Bay, Malta, on 23 September 1969, and broke in two. One member of her crew was lost.

With the assistance of the Alexandra Towing Company's steam tug *Murton*, the Bibby Line's s.s. *Leicestershire* is seen arriving at the Port of Swansea during 1964.

The *Leicestershire* was built by the Fairfield Ship Building & Engineering Co. Ltd of Govan for the Bibby Line's passenger and cargo service between the United Kingdom and Burma. The vessel entered service a year after the *Warwickshire*, completed in the same shipyard in 1948. But the *Leicestershire*'s maiden voyage was marred on the homeward journey when she was involved in a collision with a tanker in the Red Sea.

Both the *Leicestershire* and *Warwickshire* were fine looking vessels and were the first post-war passenger ships built for the Bibby Line and the first for many years in the company's fleet to be propelled by steam turbines.

The 8,922 gross ton *Leicestershire* had accommodation for 76 first-class passengers in single-, two- and three-berth cabins on the bridge and upper decks, and at the forward end of the bridge deck were two special two-berth state rooms and bathrooms. Public rooms were arranged on the

promenade deck. However, with the decline in the demand *Leicestershire* eventually ceased to carry passengers and operated as a cargo vessel only.

During 1965 both the *Leicestershire* and *Warwickshire* were sold to Typaldos Bros. Ltd, Greece. The *Leicestershire* was renamed *Iraklion* and fitted out for passenger and vehicle-ferry service, but sadly the vessel foundered in the Aegean Sea on 8 December 1966, after being overwhelmed by heavy seas. At the time the ship was on a voyage from Crete to Piraeus and of the 281 people on board only 47 survived the tragedy.

The 186 gross ton, steam tug *Murton* was built in May 1929 by Cammell Laird & Co. Ltd, Birkenhead, as the *Ceemore* for Johnston Warren Lines Ltd. After being acquired by the Alexandra Towing Co. Ltd in 1959 she was refitted on the Mersey and renamed *Murton*. The tug arrived at Swansea on Wednesday, 20 May 1959 after a 26 hour journey from Liverpool. In July 1964 she was laid up and on 20 October that year was towed by the tug *Wallasey* to Thos W. Ward Ltd, Briton Ferry, for breaking up.

The cargo ship *Enugu Palm* photographed from the pilot cutter *Seamark*, off Mumbles Head, Swansea.

The crippled British general-cargo ship *Enugu Palm* was towed safely into Swansea Docks at midnight on Thursday, 1 May 1975. The 5,141 gross ton motor vessel had been sighted drifting without power 30 miles north of the Scilly Isles on Wednesday, 30 April, following an explosion in her engine room. The ship, bound for West Africa with a miscellaneous cargo which had been loaded at Liverpool, was spotted by the crew of the *Victoria* and within some 70 minutes she was taken in tow by the Swansea based tug of the Alexandra Towing Co. Ltd, one of the most powerful tugs operating in the Bristol Channel.

The *Enugu Palm* remained in Swansea Docks until repairs were carried out and on completion of the work the vessel continued her journey to West Africa.

The *Enugu Palm*, a gleaming new cargo ship, built by Swan, Hunter and Wigham Richardson Ltd, of Wallsend-on-Tyne, first took up a berth in the King's Dock, Swansea, in 1958. She was then something more than just a new ship—she was a symbol of a new age in maritime life. Every member of her crew of 49 had his own cabin.

As the dockside cranes dipped deep into her fine holds loading corrugated-metal sheeting for West Africa, the vessel's chief officer recalled the striking difference between life aboard ships of the modern Palm Line fleet and the vessels of his earlier days at sea. 'Then,' commented the chief officer, with reference to the 1920s, 'the ordinary members of the crew lived in the fo'c'sle. They ate there and slept there. Now they live on deck level and they have their mess-room and recreation room amid ships.'

But apart from being a very impressive looking ship, the *Enugu Palm* was also a very efficient vessel. With a dead weight of 7,930 tons, she marked the completion of a fleet expansion programme conceived in 1954.

In 1978, after spending her career sailing between the United Kingdom and West Africa, she was sold to buyers in Kuwait and renamed *Athari*. In 1982 she was sold to shipbreakers in Pakistan.

The *Aghios Spyridon*, her back broken, lying across the river Neath.

The gangway ready for lowering off the poop deck to make a passageway for tugs to pass down river.

Her back broken and her hold full of water, a veteran block-ship, once part of a Mulberry Harbour at Arromanches, is pictured (left) lying across the river Neath at Giants Grave, near Thomas Wards' shipbreaking yard. Fated to be broken up for scrap after doing her duty on D-Day, the 3,385 gross ton, Greek cargo ship *Aghios Spyridon* was towed by an ocean-going tug to Swansea and safely beached off Southend in October 1945, to await the spring tides for her last journey to the 'graveyard' of ships at Briton Ferry.

On the evening tide of Sunday, 21 October, she was towed to Briton Ferry by the Alexandra Towing Company's tugs *Brockenhurst, Wallasey* and *Herculaneum*. During mooring operations, however, the *Aghios Spyridon* swung across the river—her bows almost touching the Briton Ferry bank—and broke her back, blocking the fairway and penning up-river the tugs *Brockenhurst* and *Wallasey*. The unfortunate tugs, cut off from the sea, were tied up at Neath Abbey wharf.

The people of Briton Ferry flocked to see the only block-ship sunk in the river Neath. Amidships her plates had sprung as a result of her broken back, and the deck plates were holed and buckled. Inside and out, the vessel was coated with rust and mud, for she had been sunk to her superstructure off Arromanches beach. Her decks forward were littered with thousands of machine-gun cartridge cases, which no one had time to sweep away on D-Day or in the hectic weeks that followed. Every porthole was smashed by bullets and bomb-splinters, and the captain's cabin was scarred by fire.

As for the tugs Brockenhurst and Wallasey, which had been penned in the river by the *Aghios Spyridon*, they were freed on 3 November after Thos W. Ward Ltd had cut away an angle of the poop to clear a passage for the two vessels (see picture above, right).

The s.s. *Aghios Spyridon* was built in June 1905 by Craig Taylor and Company of Stockton.

The 10,225 gross ton *Talthybius* (ex. *Empire Evenlode*) awaiting the breakers hammers at Thos. W. Ward Ltd, Briton Ferry, 1949.

Sunk twice in Far Eastern waters during the war, once by the Japanese—who refloated and renamed her *Taruyasu Maru* for use as a troopship—and later sunk by American aircraft, the *Empire Evenlode*, loaded with a cargo of 10,000 tons of scrapped war equipment, limped into the Port of Swansea during 1949. She had left Singapore on 17 January 1949, but owing to tube trouble in her boilers it took nearly three months to cover a distance which could normally be done in just a month.

The *Empire Evenlode*, named *Talthybius* by Blue Funnel line for the Far East service, was built by Scotts in 1912. She had a remarkable war experience. After surviving the First World War the vessel was struck by a German bomb in May 1941 whilst docked at Liverpool. Following repairs she made a safe journey to Singapore where in February 1942 she was sunk during an aerial bombardment of the harbour by the Japanese. However, when the Japanese captured Singapore, they refloated her and the ship, renamed *Taruyasu Maru*, was repaired and used for trooping between Manchuria and Japan. She was later sunk by the Americans and when the allies conquered the Japanese they found the *Taruyasu Maru* lying on the bottom off the north coast of Hanshu. She was then raised and handed back to the British representatives in Hong Kong. Engineers were sent out to Singapore by the Blue Funnel Line to bring the *Empire Evenlode* back to Britain. On her return journey boiler trouble forced the vessel to dock at Cape Town in order to carry out temporary repairs.

After more than forty years at sea the two Finnish four-masted barques *Pamir* and *Passatt* arrived at Penarth Docks in October 1949 to be laid-up, their life's work apparently ended. Mums came pushing toddlers in prams, fathers carried small sons on their shoulders and old folk gazed, and numerous youngsters gathered for a closer view.

The rattling of the anchor chain from the bow of the Finnish four-masted barque *Passat* in Barry Roads on Sunday, 2 October 1949 was the signal that the beautiful ship, which had taken part in what was the last Australia to England grain race for sailing ships, had won the race. The *Passat* left Port Victoria on 1 June 1949, with 56,000 bags of wheat on board, five days after the *Pamir* (see p. 97) had sailed. Her crew included two South Wales men, Frank Davies, aged 26, an ex-Navy man of Cwmrhydceirw, Morriston, and John Braithwaite, aged 26, who had been working as a civil engineer at the Abbey Steelworks. The *Passat* finally docked at Penarth on Monday, 3 October.

Despite leaving Australia five days earlier the *Pamir* arrived back at Falmouth on Sunday, 2 October 1949, after a four-month non-stop voyage from Port Victoria, Australia, with 60,000 bags of grain aboard bound for Britain. One of the members of her crew was Mr. Roy Jenkins of Garden Village, Gorseinon, who joined the vessel at New Zealand after he had spent two years in civil employment there. He had enlisted in the Merchant Navy at the age of sixteen but later decided to settle in New Zealand. However, when he heard that the *Pamir* wanted seamen to sail to England, he gave up his job and joined the crew of thirty-five, including two women from New Zealand, wives of the First and Second Officers.

In 1951 the two vessels were sold by Erikson's to Antwerp shipbreakers, but as a result of a last-minute intervention they were purchased by Herr Heinz Schliwen. During the mid '50s the vessels were run by the Pamir and Passat Foundation and the refurbished craft made regular runs between Hamburg and Buenos Aires. In 1957, however, the *Pamir* was involved in a great tragedy. On 26 September the barque sailed into hurricane 'Carrie' off the Azores and foundered; of the 52 cadets and 34 crew on board, only six survived. Shortly afterwards the Atlantic weather struck again off the Azores when the *Passat* almost met her end. Fortunately the ship was able to reach Lisbon, but following this incident it was decided that the *Passat* would never put to sea again. Today she is well looked after, fully rigged, in the German Baltic seaport of Travemunde.

The four-masted barques *Passat*, nearest the camera, and *Pamir* at Penarth Docks, 1949.

The broken wreck of the *Amazon* on Aberavon beach, 1908.

In the early hours of Tuesday, 1 September 1908 a ship was wrecked on the shores of Swansea Bay, off Port Talbot. The 2,062 gross ton, four-masted iron barque *Amazon*, built in 1886 at Glasgow by Barclay Curle & Co., and owned by Robert Hill of Greenock, was blown from her anchorage by a ferocious gale on the Monday evening and, dragging her anchors, drifted ashore. The breakers had swept the masts away and split her hull in two. Dead and alive crew members were washed up on the beach and the crowds which thronged the shore watched in suspense the efforts made to rescue the sole survivor on board with the aid of the rocket apparatus.

The *Amazon* had only left Port Talbot on the Monday morning bound for Iquique with a cargo of 2,000 tons of coal. She was towed as far as Mumbles and left anchored off Mumbles Head. After having dragged her anchors, the vessel was swept up channel before she finally grounded on the sandy beach at Aberavon. There, this once proud vessel was pounded to pieces until the remnants that remained of the keel could hardly be recognised as having once formed part of a ship.

Onlookers felt that so long as the mizzen mast held, there was a chance of saving some of the men who had climbed the rigging. But suddenly a giant breaker caught the ship and after the spray had cleared it was evident that the remaining mast had been swept away, along with 20 people. Although barely a hundred yards separated the ship from the shore, the wind and waves were so great that nothing could be done to save those that perished.

However, during a lull in the storm, spectators caught sight of one of the crew still clinging to the stump of the mizzen mast. Several attempts were made to reach the forlorn figure who was finally rescued by Mr. Charles Russell after he had managed to swim to the ship which lay thirty yards off shore. After the survivor was brought ashore several spectators scrambled to the side of the *Amazon* and successfully rescued another member of the crew. But the brave nautical veteran, Captain Carrick, and twenty other crew members were lost. Only eight survived.

The *Amazon* was a total wreck and her cargo of coal was dispersed by the storm which had claimed not only the vessel but also so many members of her crew.

The wreck of the *Brodland*, 1913.

On Monday, 20 January 1913, the s.s. *Brodland*, laiden with 2,500 tons of coal for Puntas Arenas in the Magellan Straits, was leaving Port Talbot docks towed by the steam tug *Emily Charlotte*. On clearing the entrance channel, a sudden squall and heavy seas caused her tow rope to break and before assistance could be given the vessel was blown towards the sands in front of the Jersey Beach Hotel.

Local live-saving apparatus, under the command of Captain Humphrey Jones, harbour master of Port Talbot, was quickly on the scene in response to distress rockets fired from the *Brodland*. Initially, conditions prevented the rescue crew from establishing communication with the ship. As the tide receded, however, the rocket apparatus was brought down to the water's edge and a line was fired to the *Brodland* and secured by the crew. The first man ashore was a Chinese lamp-room fireman —Ching Guen. He was taken to the Jersey Beach Hotel where preparation were made to receive the shipwrecked mariners.

After three hours hard work, forty-two crew members were brought ashore. The last man to leave the ship was Captain Vernon, a Scotsman. The only local man aboard was Mr. F. L. James, from Tydraw Street, Aberavon, the ship's carpenter, who was on his first voyage.

As the tide receded the *Brodland* was left high and dry, broadside to the beach, embedded in the sand and with a list to port. Several of her plates were damaged, hatches and deckhouse had been swept away, and fragments of the vessel were strewn for a considerable distance along the beach. The 2,989 gross ton vessel was later deemed to be a total wreck.

Brodland was built by Craig Taylor & Co., Stockton-on-Tees, in 1891 as the *Highland Mary* for the Nelson Line. She was renamed *Brodland* in 1912, during which year she sailed on her first Blue Star voyage laden with coal, from Barry to South America.

A general view of Port Talbot Docks and Talbot wharf extension in June 1923. The vessels from left to right are: the British s.s. *Fellside*; the Greek s.s. *Niki*; the British s.s. *Machado*; the French s.s. *Arez* and *Fez*; and the Norwegian s.s. *Haugland*. The *Fellside*, was a regular trader to Port Talbot, but this was probably the last time she was photographed at the docks for she was wrecked on the Gower coast during heavy weather and thick fog before dawn in January 1924. Bound from Bordeaux to Swansea, the vessel went aground on the rocks near Three Cliffs Bay.

A resident of Three Cliffs, on being awakened by loud reports, made his way in the company of his son towards the cliffs where they found the steamship with her bows pointing landward. They immediately contacted the coastguards, based at Oxwich Bay but by the time the rescue crew and apparatus arrived on the scene the ship was found to be abandoned. Despite the heavy seas, the crew of the *Fellside* had taken to the boats and, after a hard struggle, they all managed to reach the shore at Oxwich, with the exception of one man who jumped overboard and was drowned.

The *Fellside* was owned by Messrs. W. Robson and Co., of Cardiff, and registered at Belfast. Her master was Captain S. E. Drake of Cardiff. The vessel was adjudged to be a complete wreck and was purchased by H. Greening & Sons of Killay who cut her up and sold her for scrap.

HMS *Anson*.

Swansea Bay echoed to the sound of saluting guns as the battleship HMS *Anson*, under the command of Captain M. H. Eveleigh RN, celebrated the Queen's Birthday during the ship's visit to Swansea in August 1947.

Captain Eveleigh was no stranger to Swansea. He was an officer aboard HMS *Valiant* which had anchored in the bay at the time of King George V's visit to the town in August 1920, when he laid the foundation stone of the University College.

Anson, pictured between Mumbles Head and the inner rock, was an awesome sight in the bay and many people were ferried out to look her over during an open day. Indeed, demand was so great that one of the ship's boats was pressed into service and amongst those invited on board were twenty nurses from Swansea General Hospital.

After her arrival home from the Far East during the summer of 1946, the 35,000 gross ton battleship, completed in 1942, was used as a training ship. In wartime, her complement was 2,000 officers and men. HMS *Anson* was 745 ft long with a 103ft beam and her armaments included ten 14-inch guns and sixteen 5.25-inch guns. She was scrapped in 1957.

BP *Firemaster*.

Moored alongside a small jetty in the Queen's Dock, Swansea, in 1965 was a unique vessel. With its tubular supports and imposing tower it resembled a North Sea oil rig but the twin-hulled catamaran, BP *Firemaster*, was specifically designed to provide the dock with fire-fighting cover. The highly manoeuverable fire-float had an engine arrangement enabling it to move in any direction, and seven of the nine water jets could also be used in any direction simultaneously. When in use the vessel was manned by members of the Swansea Fire Service.

The 60ft long BP *Firemaster* was built at Pembroke Dock by R. S. Hayes Ltd, in conjunction with Merry Weather & Sons Ltd. The 40 ft high tower supported two platforms and a control cabin so that water or foam could be directed on to the decks of any tanker, whether in light or loaded condition. The vessel had a pumping capacity of 3,100 gallons of water or 12,500 gallons of foam per minute.

During the late 1970s the BP *Firemaster* was purchased by Port Talbot Diving Marine Services Ltd and is now used as a self-propelled mobile crane barge, working out of the Port of Swansea.

102

Crippled by fire, the Swansea trawler *Allegiance* is towed into the docks in May 1965 by the tug *Sloyne*, whose master described the salvage operation as the most difficult task he had undertaken during his forty years at sea. An electrical fault was believed to have set the trawler ablaze south of Caldey Island, off Tenby, and, after a ninety-minute battle to contain the flames, the trawler was abandoned by skipper Mr. Jonathan Hodge of Vivian Road, Swansea, mate Mr. Ronnie Fletcher of Gendros Avenue East, and crewmen Mr. Harry Wright of Fleet Street, and Mr. Brian Jeffries of Mumbles. They were picked up by the Swedish ore carrier *Saggat* and transferred to the Tenby lifeboat. The Trinity House vessel *Alert*

and the Alexandra Towing Company tug *Sloyne*, skippered by Captain Jim Screech, doused the trawler using hoses and the tug then towed her into Swansea Docks. At one stage, the trawler fuel tanks exploded, sending flames thirty feet into the air.

The 300 gross ton *Sloyne* was built by J. Crichton & Co. Ltd, of Saltney, Chester in 1928. Before arriving in Swansea on 15 May 1962, she spent most of her time working at Southampton. In October 1965 she was laid-up at the Prince of Wales Dock before being sold in 1966 to C. Brand & Company of Belfast and renamed *Lavinia*. She was broken-up at Cork in 1969.

103

Ex HMS *Nile* passing through the King's Dock Lock, Swansea, 1912.

The opening of the King's Dock also prompted the development of a new industry, that of ship-breaking, and vessels, particularly obsolete battleships, were often seen making their last voyage to Swansea.

The ex. HMS *Nile* arrived at the King's Dock Lock on July 1912 for breaking-up at the yard of Messrs Thos W. Ward Ltd. For a few days the *Nile* had been lying in Swansea Roads, the weather and anchor trouble having prevented her from docking. However, she finally reached her destination with the aid of five tugs, an operation witnessed by large crowds.

The *Nile* was built in 1888 at a cost of about £750,000. She was heavily armoured having plates 18-20 inches thick. The vessel, purchased for £30,000, was at the time the largest battleship bought for 'scrapping'.

The *Uruguay* berthing in the King's Dock, Swansea, 1942.

When the 20,183 gross ton s.s. *Uruguay* docked at Swansea on 18 August 1942 she was the largest ship to have been handled by the port. With the assistance of the Alexandra Towing Company's steam tugs *Brockenhurst, Waterloo* and *Herculaneum* (nearest to the camera) she was berthed at No. 3 Quay, King's Dock. On board were 6,318 members of the United States armed forces, and following disembarkation they were dispatched from the docks, to destinations throughout Great Britain, by main line trains brought to the ship's side. This was the forerunner of many similar disembarkations and an enviable reputation was built up by the Port of Swansea for its efficient handling of troop disembarkations and embarkations.

The *Uruguay* was built in January 1928 by Virginia's Newport News Shipbuilding and Dry-dock Company, and completed for the Panama Pacific Line as the *California*. When built she had accommodation for 384 first- and 363 tourist-class passengers. In 1938 she underwent extensive alterations and modernisation; her after funnel was removed and her forward funnel replaced by a wide single funnel, and her name was changed from *California* to *Uruguay*.

In 1941 she was taken over by the United States Navy and fitted out as a troop transporter, and painted grey. The *Uruguay* underwent another conversion in 1947 and emerged with new passenger accommodation and greatly enlarged crew quarters. She was withdrawn from service in 1954 and returned to her US Government owners, who laid her up with the reserve fleet in James River, Virginia. In November 1963 the vessel was sold to the North American Smelting Co., Wilmington, Delaware for breaking-up.

The *Gyda-C* making her way into Swansea, 1974.

Many of those interested in shipping and who are able to recall events relating to World War II are sure to remember the legendary convoy HX84, better known as the Jervis Bay Convoy. In April 1974 the *Gyda-C*, the last surviving vessel from the 38 merchantmen making up the wartime Jervis Bay Convoy, arrived at the King's Dock, Swansea, to load a 5,000 ton cargo of coal bound for Italy.

In 1940 *Gyda-C*, then named *Cetus* and flying the Norwegian flag, formed part of HX84 which encountered the German pocket battleship, *Admiral Sheer*, in mid-Atlantic. The *Cetus* and all but five of the convoy escaped the German guns, but the *Jervis Bay*, which had been converted into an armed commerce protection cruiser, fought to her last gun and went down with most of her crew, including her master, Captain Fogarty Fegen.

The *Gyda-C*, originally a steamship, was built by Murdock and Murray Ltd, of Glasgow as the *Motto* and delivered in April 1920 to Pelton S.S. Company of Newcastle-upon-Tyne. She traded as a mail boat between the Scottish Islands and Ireland until 1936, when the vessel was sold and renamed *Cetus*. During the mid 1950s the ship was rebuilt and altered and became a motor vessel. It acquired the name *Gyda-C* in 1966 after being purchased by H. F. Cordes and Co., Hamburg. The *Gyda-C* continued to trade until 1979 when she was broken up at Trieste.

The *Flying Kestrel*. The Mumbles lifeboat, *William Gammon*, can also be glimpsed in the background.

The steam tug *Flying Kestrel*, pictured in Swansea Bay during 1967, was built by Henry Scarr Ltd of Heasle, near Hull in May 1943 as the *Empire Mascot*, one of the large class of coast-wise tugs built for the Ministry of War Transport.

During 1947 she was bought by Metal Industries Ltd, and renamed *Metinda IV*, registered at the Port of Glasgow. Two years later she passed into the ownership of the Alexandra Towing Co. Ltd and was renamed *Flying Kestrel*—the fourth tug to carry the name; the first having been built in 1878 as the 135 gross ton *Narwhal* and acquired by the Alexandra Towing Company in 1887.

The *Flying Kestrel* saw service at Liverpool, Southampton and Swansea where she arrived in February 1965, only to return to Liverpool the same year. In June 1966, however, she returned to Swansea where she worked until sold in 1969 by the Alexandra Towing Co. Ltd to Haulbowline Industries, Passage West, Cork for breaking up. The 244 gross ton vessel was towed out of Swansea by the tug *Mumbles* on 17 March 1969.

The *Sobrietas* being towed out of Swansea by the tug *Mumbles*, 1970.

A sad sight for shiplovers as the 15,000 gross ton tanker *Sobrietas*, which had been taken into Milford Haven, and later Swansea, in February 1970, after being seriously damaged in a storm at sea, sets off on her final voyage to Spain and the scrapyard. The fateful blow was delivered in early February when high winds and rough seas combined to tear a huge hole in the tanker's port side, whilst on route to the Persian Gulf. The only option open to the vessel's master was to head for the nearest port in order to discharge a cargo of highly inflammable naptha. This was accomplished at the Esso jetty, Milford Haven.

After having unloaded at Milford Haven the *Sobrietas* set sail for the Prince of Wales dry dock at Swansea. But her troubles were not over. Off Mumbles Head she was almost grounded on the Mixon Sands and on arrival at Swansea her torn plates were the cause of a few anxious moments as docking operations began. The storm damage had increased the ship's 70ft beam by ten feet, leaving no room to spare as the *Sobrietas* negotiated gates 86ft wide. Even after being repaired the 11,302 gross ton *Sobrietas*, built by Lithgows Ltd, Port Glasgow, in 1953, was deemed to be unseaworthy, and was sold to Spanish shipbreakers. She left Swansea in March 1970.

The *Boelbec*.

One morning in 1942, in complete darkness, the 1,342 gross ton *Bolbec* was making for the Thames when she was in collision with a large Dutch vessel. As a result of the collision sea-water poured through a hole in the side of the *Bolbec*'s No. 2 hold. Then, the cargo shifted and the vessel heeled over on her port side. In the ensuing minutes her master, Captain W. S. Bie of Cardiff, realising that the *Bolbec* was doomed, fired distress rockets, and the order was given to abandon ship. The starboard lifeboat was launched. Out of the crew of twenty-three, twenty were saved by a passing drifter. Three men were unfortunately lost.

For seven and a half months the *Bolbec* lay on the sea bed but, eventually, salvage operations carried out by the Port of London Authority ended in her being towed about 20 miles under water on her side to Southend, where she was beached and put upright. The vessel was temporarily repaired, floated and towed to Gravesend. Here, such was her appearance, with mud-coated sides and decks, and twisted iron-work, that the cargo of coal which was being discharged appeared to be emerging direct from the bowels of Mother Earth.

But despite her condition the ship's owners, Messrs. Harris Bros, of Swansea, decided to have the *Bolbec* repaired. Tenders were invited from several firms, but these were turned down. Captain Bie and his crew, however, were more determined. They offered to clear the vessel themselves. Their offer was accepted by the owners but it took them eighteen months. At the end of a year and a half the clean-up job was so good that the *Bolbec* was able to proceed under her own steam to the Tyne for permanent repairs. This work was subsequently delayed by the Ministry of War Transport, but eventually the ship was completely re-modernised and put back into service. The vessel was finally sold to Dutch shipbreakers in 1958.

An official inspection of the Port of Swansea, 1928.

With the sole aim of boosting trade some 200 representatives of leading shipping, manufacturing and other firms based at Liverpool, London and the Midlands, together with an accompanying press corp, were conveyed to the Port of Swansea in June 1928 by the Great Western Railway Company. The party, which included the chairman of the GWR Company and other board members, were brought to the docks by private coaches from the station. There they were joined by dock officials and, following an inspection of the tinplate shipment sheds and other dock-side installations, the party boarded tugs for a guided tour of the entire dock system: the coal shipment wharves, with special appliances for the handling of anthracite coal; the King's Dock with its facilities for dealing with general cargoes; and the Queen's Dock devoted almost exclusively to the oil trade.

Official opening of the Prince of Wales Dock extension, Swansea, 1898.

On Friday, 11 March 1898, the Prince of Wales Dock extension was formerly opened, thereby providing increased facilities for the import and export trade centred upon the Port of Swansea. Tenders for the extension were authorised by Parliament in 1894, and were invited in the spring of 1895. The tender submitted by Sir John Jackson of Westminster was accepted by the trustees in January 1896 and construction work began in February. On completion, the surface water area at ordinary spring-tide level was increase by 4 ¼ acres and the effective length of quay frontage increased by about 2,000ft.

The town's elité assembled in the vicinity of the space set aside at the east end of the new extension for the opening ceremony. The ladies, taking full advantage of the glorious weather, came regaled in their prettiest costumes; vessels and buildings alike were bedecked with flags and bunting, and in the vicinity of the new facility many thousands of people gathered to witness the historic event.

At the appointed time, 11.30a.m., the carriage carrying the Marquis and Marchioness of Worcester drew alongside the space allotted for laying the foundation stone. The distinguished couple were formally welcomed by the Mayor and Mayoress, Sir John Jenkins, MP and Lady Jenkins. Sir John Jackson then presented her ladyship with an inscribed silver trowel who duly declared the stone 'well and truly laid'.

The *Michel Swenden* aground on Aberavon beach, 1957.

The 500 gross ton motor coaster *Michel Swenden* had journeyed unladen from Waterford with the intention of taking on-board a cargo of coal at Port Talbot, before proceeding to Ghent, Holland. But the plan was thwarted when the vessel went aground on Aberavon beach, off the north-west breakwater pier on Saturday, 2 February 1957. The coaster had been waiting outside the entrance to Port Talbot for a pilot to come aboard, when her anchor was torn away and the vessel swept inshore.

Attempts to refloat the *Michel Swenden*, left high and dry by the receding tide with its master, Captain Willem Bakker of Antwerp, and crew

aboard, soon attracted large crowds, and buses to the beach were packed with sightseers who took advantage of a fine Saturday evening to watch the tugs at work. Despite the use of bulldozers, called upon to carry out vital prepartory work, the attempt to refloat the ship on the evening of Sunday, 3 February, proved unsuccessful. The vessel finally made her escape with the aid of the tugs *Harrington, Waterloo* and *Wallasey* on the evening of 14 February.

The *Michel Swendon* changed her name to *Michel* in 1964 and was broken up at Hoogezand, Holland five years later.

Four tugs attempting to free the *Orelia*, Aberavon Beach, 1954.

Many hundreds of visitors at Aberavon beach watched the iron-ore vessel *Orelia* pass by one Saturday evening in August 1954, before coming to a sudden halt at the harbour mouth at Port Talbot. What they did not know was that the vessel, owned by the Holder Brothers and carrying a 9,000 ton cargo of ore loaded at Oxelosund, Sweden, had gone aground. The following morning four tugs tried unsuccessfully to free the vessel that had

been left high and dry for 24 hours. Twelve hours later, however, five tugs of the Alexandra Towing Company, namely the *Langland, Waterloo, Alexandra, Herculaneum* and *Brockenhurst*, eventually freed the *Orelia* which later docked at Port Talbot.

In 1972 the vessel was sold to Orelia Star Shipping of Limassol, and two years later was broken-up in Spain.

Mumbles lifeboat coxswain Derek Scott was awarded the RNLI's Silver Medal and his crewmen each received an inscribed vellum certificate in recognition of their gallantry in taking the crew off the Dutch coaster *Kilo*, following a fire on board the vessel in November 1963. The incident occurred when the 571 gross ton *Kilo* was bound for Rotterdam with a cargo of cotton, barrels of grease, whisky, gas cylinders, and a deck cargo of two caravans and sodium drums. A south-west gale gusting to storm force ten not only battered the vessel but also damaged some of the drums containing the highly inflammable substance which instantly caught fire. Needless to say that attempts by the crew to wash the sodium off the deck only increased the flames.

About 35 miles south of the Smalls lighthouse the *Kilo* altered course for Swansea and the rescue services were alerted. The Padstow, Tenby and Mumbles lifeboats were launched, the latter being guided through the darkness to the blazing vessel, located some eight miles south-west of Mumbles Head, by the light of flares dropped by a Shackelton aircraft. Some one and a half hours after being sighted the *Kilo* reached the comparative calm and safety of Swansea Bay, where the pilot cutter *Seamark*, equipped with fire-fighting pumps, and the lifeboat were standing by. After the coaster had beached herself off Oystermouth the fire spread to the holds containing spirits, grease and acetone. The captain had no alternative but to abandon his ship, the crew boarding the lifeboat by the light of the flames. Following the rescue operation, performed under the most difficult circumstances, the Mumbles lifeboat with the crew aboard made for the slipway at Mumbles Pier, but rough seas prevented her putting the men ashore.

In the meantime, a thunderstorm with heavy rain damped down the fire, and the Master and Chief Engineer reboarded the *Kilo*. On discovering that the engines could be restarted the vessel began to make her way to Swansea Docks, closely escorted by the *Seamark*, the Mumbles lifeboat and the Tenby lifeboat. The crew also reboarded the ship thereby allowing the lifeboat to return to the Mumbles Station. The *Kilo* was finally safely berthed at B Shed, King's Dock, Swansea.

The Dutch coaster *Kilo* safely berthed in the River Tawe, near the entrance to the South Dock after the ten-hour fire drama.

The aftermath of the South Dock fire, 1946. Sailors from the naval vessels in the background helped to extinguish the flames.

In June 1946 crowds witnessed a Swansea dock-side drama as sailors fought side by side with firemen to extinguish a fire which roared through No 22 Shed at the South Dock. The alarm had been raised by a GWR police constable and a member of the Sea Scouts but within an hour of the outbreak the shed, used by the Royal Navy as a stores, and a Naffi canteen was practically gutted. Hundreds of people, attracted by the sounds of fire engines racing down Wind Street and by a high column of smoke billowing above the South Dock, converged on the scene where they were held at bay by the police. Some onlookers also crowded on to the railway embankment above the blazing shed but

they too were ushered away by the police as the fire set nearby railway trucks ablaze.

In addition to the hazard posed by the fire itself, the fire fighters were confronted by the danger posed by exploding oil drums and blazing tins of paint. Ironically, thousands of cigarettes also went up in smoke, along with a large stock of chocolates.

Men of the Fire Service were aided by members of the crew of three minesweepers, HMS *Poole*, *Whitehaven* and *Parsborough*, moored alongside, but, because of the nature of the stored material, it soon became apparent that nothing could be done to save the shed and its contents.